RMS QUEEN ELIZABETH 2

(1967–2008)

COVER IMAGE: *QE2* **passes the Needles on the Isle of Wight.**

First published in December 2016

A catalogue record for this book is available from the British Library.

ISBN 978 085733 216 5

Library of Congress control no. 20169930196

Published by Haynes Publishing,
Sparkford, Yeovil,
Somerset BA22 7JJ, UK.
Tel: 01963 440635
Int. tel: +44 1963 440635
Website: www.haynes.com

Haynes North America Inc.,
859 Lawrence Drive, Newbury Park,
California 91320, USA

Printed in Malaysia

Commissioning Editor: Jonathan Falconer
Copy editor: Simon Fletcher
Proof reader: Penny Housden
Indexer: Peter Nicholson
Page design: James Robertson

RMS QUEEN ELIZABETH 2

(1967–2008)

Owners' Workshop Manual

An insight into the design, construction and operation
of the world's most famous ocean liner

Dr Stephen M. Payne OBE RDI

Queen Elizabeth 2 (QE2)
under way at speed.
(Michael Gallagher Collection)

Contents

Foreword

by Commodore Ronald Warwick
Master, *Queen Elizabeth 2*

When the *Queen Elizabeth 2* (*QE2*) was introduced into service in 1969, she was vastly different in appearance from the earlier Cunarders and those liners of other notable shipping companies. The 'new look' was a surprise to many, but within a year her more streamlined hull, along with her contemporary interior design, gained in favour and popularity. One of the most significant design features of the *QE2* was her dual role as a liner and a cruise ship – Cunard Line's response to the growing interest in the leisure market.

During the life of the *QE2* the ownership and management of the Cunard Line changed several times, and with each change came some form of modification to the vessel. Over

the years millions of pounds were spent on refurbishment, new restaurants and the addition of new cabins. Behind the scenes the steam turbines were replaced by a diesel-electric power plant, whilst the bridge was kept up to date with the most modern navigational aids and communication systems.

Dr Stephen Payne the author, naval architect and designer of the *Queen Mary 2*, will give you a perspective like no other author. More importantly, however, his book will give readers an insight into how the ship was constructed, which is quite different to those methods described in his previous book of the more modern *QM2*.

Majestically, the *QE2* sailed the seas and oceans of the world generating happy memories for the hundreds of thousands of passengers and crew who sailed aboard her. Memories shared by my family and friends are filled with nostalgia for my late father Bil Warwick, her first Captain, and sentimentality for my own association with the ship, serving first as a junior officer for many years before achieving my dream of Captain of this magnificent liner.

The Haynes *RMS Queen Elizabeth 2 Manual* is a fitting memento to the history of the liner that I am very honoured and proud to have been a part of. I congratulate and thank Stephen Payne for this important contribution to British maritime history.

Commodore R.W. Warwick
OBE, LLD, MNM
Somerset, September 2016

Acknowledgements

In writing such a book as this Haynes Owners' Manual of RMS *Queen Elizabeth 2*, there are many people to thank who have graciously given their time, photographs, memorabilia and illustrations for illustrative purposes.

I would first like to thank my friend Ronald Warwick for agreeing to write the Foreword. I've been privileged to have known Ron for many years, in fact long before Carnival Corporation (the company with which I worked) bought Cunard Line and *Queen Elizabeth 2*. However, our greatest association was during the building of *Queen Mary 2* when Ron was the designated first Master and I was the Naval Architect. Over the years it has been marvellous to sit with Ron and discuss the maritime scene, and especially to mull over aspects of *Queen Elizabeth 2* and *Queen Mary 2* design and operation. His stories are celebrated and sometimes poignant, but always informative and eminently knowledgeable.

A close second for those in line for thanks is Michael Gallagher, Cunard Line's Public Relations Manager and Historian. Michael is probably *QE2*'s most ardent fan, and his depth of knowledge, experience of the ship and Cunard Line is legendary. Michael graciously assisted me with texts related to and illustrations of the ship.

Louis-Philippe Capel is a photographer and film producer whom I met whilst overseeing the design and construction of *Queen Mary 2*. Louis-Philippe was working on a promotional film about *QM2* when we met and exchanged views about passenger ship design. During his work on the *QM2* project, Louis-Philippe sailed on board *Queen Elizabeth 2* and documented her unique personality through a large number of high-quality photographs, which he kindly made available for use in this book.

Bruce Peter is a well-known author of design-inspired maritime books and is a Research Supervisor at the Glasgow School of Art. Bruce kindly dug into his collection of *QE2* photos for this book.

I am most grateful to Rob Lightbody at www.theqe2story.com and Michael Pocock at www.maritimequest.com for putting me in touch with Tony and Blair Skilton, Richard Ward and Peter Williams, who have very kindly allowed their photographs of *Queen Elizabeth 2* – both inside and out – to be used in this book.

My good friends Gordon Bauwens and his wife Christine are aficionados of *Queen Elizabeth 2*. Gordon worked as a draughtsman at the John Brown Shipyard at Clydebank before becoming an accomplished marine artist. Gordon

and Christine commemorated *QE2*'s last visit to the Clyde in 2008 by taking a number of magnificent photographs before putting paint to canvas for a marvellous painting, of which I have a copy. Gordon and Christine were only too pleased to allow their pictures to appear in the book.

Family and friends always provide encouragement for projects such as this, and my thanks go to my dear friend Jennifer, my mother Pauline and three younger brothers. With two of my brothers I accompanied our parents on a day trip visit to the *QE2* in June 1969 when she was barely a month old. As a nine-year-old, little did I know that nearly 50 years later I would be writing an Owners' Manual about her! Regardless to say, I am saddened that my late father won't see this book, but at least he was able to see the *Queen Mary 2* volume before being cruelly taken by Alzheimer's in 2015. He is fondly remembered by us all, and his legacy of that *QE2* visit in 1969 was taking a cherished cine film of the day.

Thanks are also due to Jonathan Falconer, first for commissioning the Haynes *Queen Mary 2* Manual, and this one too. His encouragement and help, and above all patience, are very much appreciated, and I sincerely hope that we have the opportunity of working together on other projects in the future.

BELOW Gordon and Christine Bauwens with some of Gordon's paintings displayed on board *QE2*, 5 October 2008. *(Yvonne Bauwens Collection)*

Introduction

20 September 1967. I distinctly remember television news showing the launch of a great new ship. In the grainy black and white television images the hull was seen thundering down the slipway, to be noisily brought to rest by a collective of massive drag chains after Her Majesty Queen Elizabeth II had named the liner *Queen Elizabeth the Second – QE2.*

BELOW A fine study of *Queen Elizabeth 2* as delivered after dieselisation. *(Louis-Philippe Capelle Collection)*

Wimbledon fortnight, 1969. It was warm and sunny. The Payne family, comprising parents Michael and Pauline and their three sons Stephen (aged 9), Alan (aged 6) and Victor (aged 4), were on their annual summer holiday at their beloved south coast resort of Boscombe, just outside Bournemouth. Amongst the favoured activities, apart from building sandcastles on the splendid sandy beach, was sailing motorised Sutcliffe tinplate model boats and a Nautilus clockwork

submarine on a small model boat pond at Boscombe cliff gardens.

Thirty-two miles away in Southampton's Ocean Dock lay Cunard Line's new transatlantic liner, *Queen Elizabeth 2*. The ship had only entered service a few weeks earlier and had already gained notoriety for the lengthy delays in bringing her into commission, owing to extensive mechanical problems and outfitting woes. Cunard had invested everything in the ship and the future of the company rested

solely on her success – or failure. Back in Boscombe, the Payne family chanced across a street advertising placard that offered a coach trip visit to Southampton docks and a tour of *Queen Elizabeth 2*. Off we went, boarding *QE2* via Ocean Terminal, the superlative art deco terminal built for the former two *Queens* and completed in 1950, sadly demolished in 1983. My two brothers and I were in shorts and summer shirts – I also wore a smart brown jacket. Father wore a vibrant orange towelling polo-type shirt, whilst Mother wore a two-piece, pale blue Crimplene ensemble. Crimplene was the new wonder synthetic fabric of the age, being crease-proof, with no ironing required, and durable. Mother's garment was highly appropriate for a visit on board *Queen Elizabeth 2* as the ship heralded the onset of the modern era, where wood panelling was eschewed and replaced by plastic, brass was supplanted by chrome and pomp was displaced by chic. It was a memorable visit in so many ways, not least in cementing an enduring love affair with *Queen Elizabeth 2*. Father had his 8mm cine camera with him and took a precious few minutes of film to record the day. It shows us sitting in the First Class Columbia Restaurant and the Transatlantic (Tourist Class) Double Up Room. Another scene depicts us on deck with the single streamlined funnel towering above. The camera then pans to view the surrounding docks, with Royal Mail Line's eclectic cruise ship *Andes*, resplendent in her white livery and buff funnel, taking centre stage. Suddenly a long streamlined bow slowly comes into view … the sleek greyhound edges further into shot proudly displaying two immense red, white and blue funnels and a silver mast. It is none other than SS *United States*, flagship of the American merchant marine, fastest ever passenger liner and holder of the Blue Riband of the Atlantic. A memorable day indeed. As a nine-year-old I had already been interested in great liners for four years, since watching a report about the Cunard liner *Queen Elizabeth* on the BBC children's television programme *Blue Peter*, broadcast on 24 May 1965 – when I was five.

Wimbledon fortnight, 2014. Thoughts turned to that splendid day back in 1969 when I first visited *Queen Elizabeth 2*. What could have been the date? Scouring the internet,

ABOVE The author pictured on *QE2*'s top deck ahead of the mighty funnel. *(Stephen Payne Collection)*

LEFT The author's parents, Pauline and Michael, visit the *Queen Elizabeth 2* during her last year in service. *(Stephen Payne Collection)*

I chanced across a scan of QE2's maiden season schedule listing cruises and transatlantic crossings from February to November 1969; in the event several of these sailings had been cancelled because Cunard did not accept the liner into service until 18 April 1969. From this document I could deduce what days the ship was in Southampton. I also have a copy of Andrew Britton's superb book about SS *United States* which was a gift from my good friend, and fellow naval architect, Hampton Dixon. This book has a section that lists all the voyages of the ship, although only the arrival and departure dates from New York are given. Judicial analysis enabled me to estimate what dates the ship was at Southampton and a correlation with the QE2 dates could be made to home in on the probable visit date. The only occasions where the two ships seemed to appear together in Southampton in June and July were 24 and 26 July. As QE2 sailed for New York on 26 July, it's unlikely she would have entertained visitors on that day, so I assume we visited on Thursday 24 July. However, this was in conflict with my original assumption that we as a family always took our summer holiday during Wimbledon fortnight in late June. When I checked with my mother, she was horrified that I should have thought that we were taken out of school for our holidays; so I am now confident that the day was 24 July.

My first voyage on QE2 was in 1979, when I joined the ship in Cherbourg for the short cross-Channel trip back to Southampton at the conclusion of an eastbound transatlantic crossing. I travelled with my friend Zane Leo and we were allocated a First Class Boat Deck cabin for our day use. We ate in the Columbia Restaurant, where I had previously been filmed by my father during our family visit to the ship in 1969. My first proper transatlantic voyage was the 16 December departure in 1984 from Southampton to New York. The deal with Cunard included a night at the Ritz Carlton in Manhattan and, following a Christmas stopover in the American capital, a return flight from Washington DC. The voyage was not particularly memorable except for one aspect of the entertainment. This was a maritime-themed lecture where the presenter merely showed images of old liners and asked the audience to identify them. Unfortunately, this was in the era of projected slides, rather than the PowerPoint presentations that we use today, and the hapless presenter had dropped his slides immediately prior to his presentation. As a result, many of them were upside down and/or back to front. Worse still, as they were out of order and the lecturer didn't really know which ship was which, we were presented amongst others with the *Normandie* that was in fact the *Rex* and the *Bremen* that was the *Ile de France*. Affronted that such mediocre entertainment should be offered on the *Queen*, I complained to Cunard and by return was offered the chance of being a lecturer, 'If I thought I could do better'. I've been lecturing with Cunard ever since!

I made many further voyages on board *Queen Elizabeth 2*, both transatlantic crossings and cruises. All were happy trips and QE2 always seemed to step up to the mark and make them all memorable. There was another December transatlantic when the weather was so bad we were two days late arriving at New York. The drama on that voyage included one of the Columbia Restaurant windows giving way under the force of the onslaught and the resulting deluge swamping nearby tables. Regardless to say, all was dealt with efficiently and calmly, and within half an hour everything was back to normal. There was also the poignant, final transatlantic crossing in tandem with *Queen Mary 2* on 16–22 October 2008, as well as cruises to the Mediterranean, and more.

Cunard needed *Queen Elizabeth 2* to be a profitable ship from the outset, as all the company's reserves had been expended bringing her into service. Not long into her career the oil crisis of the 1970s threatened her viability as her fuel bill soared. Intensifying her operation and minimising time spent in port during turn-arounds helped the balance sheet, but as we will see, compromised her reliability. By the mid-1980s the ship was in crisis and it looked as though the diagnosis was terminal. Thankfully, a transplant in the form of complete re-engining took place in the winter of 1986/87 and a rejuvenated and revitalised *Queen* emerged. In order to keep the ship current and competitive, Cunard continued to spend vast sums of money refitting the passenger areas of the ship. From 1972 additional cabins were progressively added and public rooms were remodelled. However, on several occasions these refits were seriously mistimed, resulting in abysmal situations on board which the British tabloid press reported with relish. Despite all these problems and woes, *Queen Elizabeth 2* seemed to rise above it all, and she remained the first choice for many loyal and devoted passengers. Notice of withdrawal came as a surprise but was inevitable. The cost of keeping an ageing ship in commission without the increased revenue streams attributable to numerous balconies, lack of ship-wide internet and other financial considerations as a result of creeping obsolescence, proved too much. *Queen Elizabeth 2* remained in commission between 18 April 1969 and 27 November 2008, surpassing *Aquitania*'s 1914–49 record for the longest serving express liner in company service. As this is written, it is eight years since she made her last grand exit out of Southampton, ostensibly to become a floating hotel and leisure complex in Dubai. Despite a number of announcements, *Queen Elizabeth 2* remains moribund at the Gulf State with seemingly little prospect of any rebuilding or a return to useful purpose.

A word about the title of the book, RMS *Queen Elizabeth 2*, in particular the RMS. Michael Gallagher, Cunard's Historian and Public Relations Manager, advises that although RMS is frequently used and associated with the ship, Sir Basil Smallpiece – the Chairman of Cunard at the time of her entry into service – discouraged this, saying that it detracted from the ship's modernity.

This book is a companion volume to the author's Haynes Owners' Manual of *Queen Elizabeth 2*'s successor, *Queen Mary 2*. It describes the history of Cunard and why *Queen Elizabeth 2* was such an important element of the fleet. We look at the ship's construction and some of the technical aspects of her operation, then take a historical guided tour around her decks, highlighting the many changes that occurred. I hope that the book will be seen as a tribute to the men and women of John Brown & Co. Ltd Clydebank that built her and the splendid work that they did. *Queen Elizabeth 2* was sadly the last liner to be built on the Clyde. She was a great ship and I doubt we'll ever see her like again built on UK shores. Long live the *Queen*!

Stephen M. Payne
OBE RDI MNM FRINA FREng
Designer Cunard Line *Queen Mary 2*
Past President the Royal Institution of Naval Architects

June 2016

BELOW *QE2*'s last day in Southampton, 11 November 2008. *(Stephen Payne Collection)*

Chapter One

Cunard and the North Atlantic Ferry

Since the introduction of the diminutive paddle steamer *Britannia* in 1840, Cunard ships had crossed the great expanse of the western ocean; the Atlantic. Through wars and peace these ships had offered the inimitable Cunard standard of service. Yet, as the late 1950s dawned, Cunard needed a new ship to maintain its cherished traditions. But there was a problem: the jet airliner had appeared to challenge their supremacy. Nobody at Cunard took this threat seriously, however.

OPPOSITE The new *Queen Mary* sails down the Clyde having just departed the John Brown Shipyard, 24 March 1936. *(Bruce Peter Collection)*

Following the cessation of hostilities at the end of the Second World War, commercial shipping gradually returned to normal service. However, many ships were retained in Government service for a considerable period of time to repatriate displaced persons and return troops home. One of the first ships released was Cunard Line's 83,000grt *Queen Elizabeth* (1940), which had never previously entered commercial service. She spent some time refitting at Southampton before moving up to anchor in the River Clyde for completion of the work to transform her from troopship to premier ocean liner. On 16 October 1946 she departed on her maiden voyage from Southampton bound for New York, where she arrived five days later. The reconditioned 81,000grt *Queen Mary* (1936) joined her running mate in service on 31 July 1947, when Cunard's dream of a two-ship, weekly transatlantic service, first envisaged in 1927, finally became a reality. Cunard successfully marketed *Queen Mary* as the fastest ship in the world, whilst *Queen Elizabeth* was promoted as the largest liner in the world.

Thereafter, the two Cunard *Queens* dominated the Atlantic ferry since all the pre-war fliers had succumbed to the hostilities. French Line's superlative 80,000grt *Normandie* (1935) had been destroyed following a fire whilst outfitting as a troopship in New York on 9 February 1942; North German Lloyd's *Bremen* (1929) was similarly lost by fire in 1941,

whilst their *Europa* (1930) was ceded to France, only to sink following collision with the wreck of the former liner *Paris* in Le Havre in 1946, thus seriously delaying her Atlantic return under the Tricolour until 1950; finally, Italian Line's *Conte di Savoia* (1932) and *Rex* (1932) were both sunk following Allied air raids on Malamocco and Trieste in Italy 1943/44. On 3 July 1952 United States Lines introduced the heavily state-subsidised *United States*. At 51,000grt she was considerably smaller than the Cunard *Queens* but she had the distinction of being by far the fastest liner in the world, and captured the Blue Riband from *Queen Mary* for the fastest transatlantic crossing on her maiden voyage. Speed was always a tremendous cachet and *United States* was an instant hit, although she was never a commercial proposition.

In 1956, under the chairmanship of Colonel Denis Bates, Cunard began to seriously consider the future of its express transatlantic service; the Line's ten liners and cruise ship *Caronia* were all sailing at capacity with more people than ever travelling transatlantic by sea and air. *Queen Mary* had been in commission for 20 years and would need replacement within the next decade; with new constructions taking about four years to complete, Cunard was being prudent. After numerous design studies a new 75,000grt transatlantic liner design designated Q3 (third *Queen*-type ship) was progressed; slightly smaller than the *Queen*

'Q3' – The ship that never was! – R Pearson – 11/03.

she would replace, but a three-class Atlantic thoroughbred nonetheless. This was deemed to be the smallest and slowest vessel that could fulfil the year-round transatlantic role and offer the requisite level of Cunard hospitality and service. Although the Line had built up substantial reserves secured on the success of both their passenger and cargo operations, the escalating price of new-buildings following the Second World War dictated that a substantial loan would be required. That year the passenger fleet made a profit of £2 million, but thereafter profits began to decline steadily and by 1961 passenger operations were running at a loss. On 26 October 1958 the first non-stop

transatlantic flights began with Boeing 707 airliners; travellers could now cross the Atlantic in several hours by air compared to sailing by ship over a number of days. Competitive pricing fed burgeoning demand as air quickly became the preferred choice for many travellers.

Despite the gloomy outlook Cunard still persisted with its 'big' ship, as the Line had determined very naively that the transatlantic air phenomenon was going to be a transient blip. In 1959 Cunard approached the British Government for a loan to enable them to build Q3. Precedents had previously been set with *Lusitania/Mauretania* in 1907 (£2.6 million), *Queen Mary* in 1936 (£4.5 million) and *Queen*

ABOVE Abandoned single-purpose Q3. *(Michael Gallagher Collection)*

BELOW *Lusitania* at speed on sea trials off the Isle of Arran, early July 1907. *(Bruce Peter Collection)*

Elizabeth in 1940 (£5 million). The Conservative Macmillan Government reacted by forming a committee chaired by the industrialist Oliver Lyttelton, 1st Viscount Chandos (Lord Chandos), which reported in 1960.

Parts of the summary of the report read:

After long discussions with our professional advisers and with the Cunard Company, we have come to the conclusion – and the Cunard Company agree – that a ship having the following characteristics would best and most economically replace the 'Queen Mary' and maintain the British express passenger service across the North Atlantic:

Gross tonnage: 75,000 tons.
Service Speed: 29½kts.
Length overall: 990ft.
Beam: 114ft.
Draught: 30ft 3in.
Passenger capacity: 2,270.

Our advice is that the cost of such a ship would be between £25 million and £28 million, though Cunard think it will probably be higher. Since Cunard have available only £12 million from their own resources to invest in the project, the Government would have to provide the remainder of the capital cost. We have agreed with the Cunard Company that if the Government should decide to do so, the financial arrangements which would best safeguard the interests of the taxpayer on the one hand and the Company on the other would seem to be as follows: –

Cost

(a) The agreement would be subject to the capital cost not exceeding £30 million.

Ownership

(b) The ship would be owned and operated by the Cunard Company through a separate Company to which the Cunard Company would subscribe £12 million as equity capital. The remainder of the cost, not exceeding £18 million, would be provided by the Government as loan capital. Alternatively, the ship could be owned and/or operated by the Cunard Company so long as the Government were left in the same position as regards security and redemption as if the ship were owned by a separate Company.

H.M. Government's Loan Interest

(c) The loan would bear interest at 4½ per cent. per annum from the date on which the ship comes into service.

Redemption

(d) The loan would be redeemed by the operation of a 4½ per cent. sinking fund over twenty-five years.

(e) If the gross yield on the Cunard equity exceeds an average of 7 per cent., the excess would go to accelerate redemption of the Government loan.

(f) Cunard would have the right to redeem the outstanding balance at par at any time on reasonable notice.

Depreciation

(g) Depreciation would be at a rate of one-twenty-fifth of the capital cost per annum.

Chandos Committee Report,
Hansard, 1 June 1960

What wasn't mentioned in this summary is that a three-class structure designated First, Cabin and Tourist was recommended to be made a condition of any loan. The Committee also insisted that the transatlantic service be maintained year round, with no off-season cruising. Previously the Peninsular and Oriental Steam Navigation Company (P&O Line) and Orient Line had been considering their own requirements for new tonnage, which would ultimately take shape as the *Canberra* and *Oriana*. P&O had approached Cunard with the notion of sharing a ship, which could be used on the Atlantic during the summer months when business was still good, switching to the Australian run in the winter when that route experienced high demand. Cunard rebuffed this idea, stating that express liners designed for the transatlantic route were unsuitable for any other form of deployment. This is reflected in the comment that the ship 'would be of a size and speed which would make it unsuitable for any other service'. In 1960 the Government agreed to an £18 million loan at 4.5% interest.

Colonel Bates died shortly after the Chandos Committee reported and he was succeeded by Sir John Brocklebank, a veteran of cargo ship operations. At this time the order for Q3 was due to be placed with a Tyneside consortium made up of Vickers Armstrong and Swan Hunter and Wigham Richardson. Sir Basil Smallpeice assumed control of a company struggling to come to terms with changing trading conditions; the old guard were not prepared to accept consideration of anything other than Q3, whilst a growing element considered that a ship that couldn't undertake off-season cruising would be suicidal. Brocklebank was firmly in the sceptic camp, and after evaluation of the latest trading conditions he persuaded the Cunard Board to cancel the project outright. The announcement of this in 1961 shocked the maritime community. However, within a short time it became known that the company was looking at the design of a smaller 58,000grt dual-purpose ship that could be flexible in her operation, switching between transatlantic service and off-season cruising. When the design of Q3 was developed, it was considered that a ship of 75,000grt was the smallest that could be built to incorporate the machinery that would deliver the required performance and provide the necessary earning potential. The design was based upon a quadruple screw, steam turbine-driven ship. However, by the early 1960s it was realised that naval architecture and marine engineering had advanced to the point where a twin-screw liner could be contemplated, with a considerably more compact machinery installation; Orient Line's new 27.5kt 42,000grt *Oriana* (1961) and P&O Line's 45,000grt *Canberra* demonstrated what could be achieved. Accordingly, following the debacle of the abandonment of the single-purpose full transatlantic liner Q3, the dual-purpose Q4 was born with the following preliminary particulars:

LEFT Sir John Brocklebank, Chairman of Cunard 1959–65. *(Michael Gallagher Collection)*

BELOW The Q3 in an early stage of development with conventional funnel. *(Bruce Peter Collection)*

BOTTOM The final form of Q3 with slender funnel. *(Bruce Peter Collection)*

Length	960ft
Beam	104ft
Draught	31ft
Passengers	2,000 in three classes
Crew	1,000
Propulsion	Twin-screw, double-reduction steam turbine
Power	120,000shp
Service speed	28.5kts
Gross tonnage	58,000

ABOVE The dual-purpose Q4. (Bruce Peter Collection)

As the design of Q4 progressed the eventual working arrangements of the ship were considered, and it was estimated that with 110,000shp the fuel consumption would be 492 tons per day, half that of the existing *Queens*. In July 1964 five shipbuilding concerns were invited to tender for construction of the ship: Harland & Wolff, Belfast – builder of P&O's *Canberra*; Cammell Lairds of Birkenhead on the Mersey – builder of Union Castle Line's flagship *Windsor Castle* (1960; 38,000grt); Fairfields on the Clyde – builder of Canadian Pacific Line's *Empress of Britain* (1956; 25,516grt); John Brown Shipyard on the Clyde – builder of numerous Cunard liners including the two existing *Queens*; and finally the Swan Hunter and Wigham Richardson, builders of *Mauretania* (1907), and Vickers Armstrong consortium that had developed the abandoned Q3 design with Cunard. Cammell Lairds and Fairfields subsequently withdrew, leaving the

remaining shipyards to submit their bids towards the end of November. The submitted tenders were well above Cunard's own estimates and necessitated some cost-saving measures, such as the elimination of an aft cargo hatch and one boiler. As it turned out, the latter was a serious false economy that would have serious consequences for the operation of the ship and threaten her very existence.

On 30 December 1964 the contract was signed with John Brown Shipyard for the construction of Q4, which was designated shipyard contract 736. The contract price of £25,427,000 was not fixed as in today's shipbuilding contracts, but was subject to escalation clauses to cover increases in the cost of materials and manpower. Additionally, the shipbuilding cost had to be paid at the outset, in order to take advantage of investment allowances worth £4 million – modern passenger ships are contracted with stage payments, up to 20% being paid during construction and the remaining 80% being payable on delivery. The upshot was that with the Government £17.6 million loan only being available on delivery, Cunard had to raise the money from the open market, and £17.6 million was borrowed from a consortium of banks at 0.5% above the Bank of England Interest Base Rate. Collateral was provided by mortgaging five of the Line's passenger ships and six cargo ships. The remaining £7.8 million was made up from the £4 million investment allowance and the remainder from Cunard's own reserves.

RIGHT Apart from some refinement of the funnel design, this model of Q4 gives an accurate glimpse of how the new *QE2* would look. (Bruce Peter Collection)

All photos Michael Gallagher Collection

BUILDING THE *QE2*

FAR LEFT The first section of keel is prepared to be lifted into position on to the keel blocks to the right.

LEFT At an early stage of construction with work progressing towards the stern of the ship.

ABOVE LEFT The lower section of the stern showing the two shaft bossings before the shafts were installed.

ABOVE The hull is almost complete with just the bow to install.

LEFT The hull nears completion with the bow still to be built up.

RIGHT The massive stern frame is hoisted into position.

FAR RIGHT The stern at an early stage of construction.

RIGHT The stern festooned with scaffolding during construction.

FAR RIGHT The rudder weighing 80 tons is hoisted into position.

BELOW The portside shaft bossing and its six-bladed propeller weighing 31 tons.

ABOVE AND BELOW Aluminium sections of the superstructure receive attention.

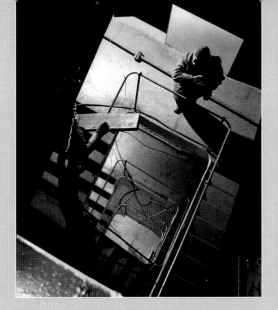

FAR LEFT A fine study of 'A' Staircase during the construction.

LEFT The boiler room begins to take shape with the open space for the uptakes for the three boilers evident at the top.

RIGHT Hoisting the wheelhouse on board.

BELOW The bulb is about to be hoisted aboard to marry up with the after contours of the forefoot.

BELOW RIGHT Launching day nears with the ship poised for her most dangerous journey – the launch itself.

Keel laying

The first keel section of the new ship was to be laid on 2 July 1965, but in the event the prefabricated 118-ton block was not put in place on the slipway until three days later, on the 5th, because of stability concerns relating to the lifting tackle. Once the section was in place construction could begin in earnest. At the time of the keel laying it was anticipated that Q4 would be delivered in May 1968, in time for the lucrative transatlantic summer season. After a six-year tenure Sir John Brocklebank resigned as Chairman of Cunard in November 1965 and was succeeded by Sir Basil Smallpeice, who had joined the Board in an executive capacity with responsibility for Cunard's London office the previous year. Sir Basil was credited with turning around the fortunes of the ailing BOAC in the early 1960s, having joined the group in 1950; he left in 1963 following a management disagreement with the Chairman. Sir Basil wasted no time in shaking up Cunard, which he felt had 'become ossified in patterns set by past success and had been living precariously on their fat until suddenly the supply ran out'. Following the recommendations of management consultants, the administration of the passenger fleet was transferred from Liverpool to London and organised into five divisions: Commercial, Hotel, Technical, Personnel and Accounting.

RIGHT Sir Basil Smallpeice, Cunard's chairman from 1965 to 1971. *(Michael Gallagher Collection)*

Cunard Line's Chairman Sir John Brocklebank said:

> *This is a very proud day for the Cunard Line and for the British shipping and shipbuilding industry. It is particularly appropriate that we should be laying the keel of the 172nd Cunarder which will be the largest passenger ship built in Britain since the Queen Elizabeth, only two days before we celebrate our 125th anniversary. And it is equally appropriate that it should be taking place here in John Brown's shipyard, the birthplace of the conspicuously successful Queens.*
>
> *In fact she will be the first large British ship to be planned and designed from the start to capture the cream of the North Atlantic trade in the season and the cream of the cruise market in the winter.*
>
> *The final result, we are sure will be a ship to match any foreseeable competitor, attractive to passengers and an economically sound investment.*

Sir John confirmed that the new liner was scheduled for launch in 1967 and that she would be in service by the spring of 1968 to take advantage of the premium summer season sailings. By that stage the company had received more than 2,000 applications for joining the ship on her maiden voyage. Cunard claimed that this was a measure of how well the liner had captured the public imagination, and that it augured well for the ship's future and that of Cunard. The company also claimed that it had received 'thousands' of suggestions for names for the ship from the public and two former Cunard liner names, namely *Aquitania* and *Berengaria*, were mentioned as strong contenders.

Sir John pointed out that 'she is far from being a scaled-down Queen liner. She will be different from anything that has gone before, not in the sense that she will contain innovations for innovation's sake, but because her design concept looks ahead into the 1970s and beyond', and that she was 'a fresh concept ship'.

Pressmen invited to the aborted launch were quickly ushered into the shipyard's model room when things went awry. Here they were liberally entertained, and fortunately the subsequent all-important press coverage was quite sympathetic towards the ship.

Sir John Brocklebank's comments regarding the dual nature of the ship's design were curious, because Canadian Pacific Line's *Empress of Britain* (42,348grt), which entered service in 1931, was a well-known exponent of such duality.

By March 1966 it was evident that the ship was at least six months behind schedule, and it was anticipated that she would be ready for launch by September 1967 with an entry into service in November 1968.

On 27 May Cunard Line issued a press announcement that had far-reaching implications for the ship.

It has also been decided, in view of the results of the Economist Intelligence Unit's market researches, that certain modifications to the ship as originally planned are desirable.

In particular, a firm decision has been taken to make the new Cunarder a two class ship. Although her original design allowed easy conversion from three classes to two classes or one, various facilities on the ship would have remained separated and the modifications are intended to concentrate these facilities where they will be most convenient. The work will include resiting or concentrating the shopping, children's and teenage areas, and combining the original cabin and tourist lounges into one large public room with a balcony.

The new Cunard Chairman, Sir Basil Smallpeice, reported:

We have chosen to revise the layout of certain passenger accommodation in the ship as well as to modify the arrangements for interior design, so as to ensure that it conforms with the new marketing policy we have evolved for our passenger business.

In travel, separate class accommodations as a reflection of a hierarchical social stature is clearly out-of-date. What is offered is a wide variety of accommodation to suit the widest possible range of demands in terms

of quality and where in traditional Cunarders, separate parts of the ship were assigned to different classes, the new ship is entirely open. All passengers can walk from end to end without let or hindrance.

JOHN BROWN ENGINEERING (CLYDEBANK) LTD: HEAVY ENGINEERING SUPPLY

Until October 1996, John Brown Engineering (Clydebank) Ltd was the engineering division of John Brown & Co. (Clydebank) Engineers and Shipbuilders – the original shipyard that built *Queen Elizabeth 2*. John Brown Engineering had been hived off to become a separate company within the John Brown Group, whereas the shipyard became the Clydebank Division of Upper Clyde Shipbuilders. It was a sad reflection on the state of British shipbuilding at the time, and it was a last-ditch attempt to secure the future of the shipyard and the others within the Group; ultimately unsuccessful.

John Brown Engineering designed (the majority of), manufactured and supplied *Queen Elizabeth 2*'s turbines, gearing, shafting, condensers, boilers, uptakes and funnel.

John Brown Engineering was acquired by Trafalgar House Investments in 1986, which in turn was taken over by Kvaerner a decade later. The Clydebank engineering works were subsequently closed in 2000, whilst the shipyard finally closed in 2001.

The site has now been cleared and Clydebank College straddles the former slipways where so many famous ships were built. The foot of the slipway remains, together with several commemorative plaques. The only other remnant from this once-thriving enterprise is the Titan crane adjacent to the fitting-out berth, which is now an observation platform for tourists.

From three- to two-class

Dan Wallace, Cunard's Chief Naval Architect who had led the Q4 design team from the start, received orders from the management to change the ship from three to two classes. By that stage the hull was almost complete, and it was Dan Wallace who made the philosophical statement that it was easier to redesign the ship with one class less than with an additional one!

On the Atlantic run, extra rooms and amenities would be available for what would now be known as Premium fare-paying passengers. The old terms First, Cabin and Tourist, so embedded in the 'Old Cunard' structure, were swept away simply by new designations of First and Tourist Classes. Later in the ship's career, Tourist would be euphemistically renamed Transatlantic Class, as a ruse to disguise its lower status.

The areas affected were primarily the public spaces, which the overall design scheme had already relegated to the uppermost strata of the ship's integral hive of passenger spaces.

RIGHT Dan Wallace, Cunard's and *QE2*'s naval architect. *(Michael Gallagher Collection)*

Deck allocation

The traditional practice of giving the highest deck to First Class was completely reversed. This was done to provide the premium fare passengers with an added measure of comfort by locating their spaces lower down in the ship, nearer the centre of gravity. Despite the use of stabilisers, Cunard was still worried about the ship's greater than normal height, particularly since the topside public spaces for each class were to include the restaurants. On North Atlantic service, First Class passengers would be assigned exclusive use of the Promenade Deck rooms whilst Tourist Class would occupy the higher Verandah and Boat Decks.

Changes to Promenade, Verandah and Boat Deck layouts

The new two-class arrangement allowed for an open plan range of passenger facilities for cruising, with provision for the two main dining rooms and a few other ancillary spaces to be segregated by class barriers during North Atlantic service only. A complete rationalisation in the layout of all public spaces, especially those originally allocated to the two lower classes (Cabin and Tourist), was also undertaken. Extra space was gained through the inevitable resultant rationalisation in the number of public rooms and associated service spaces that would be required.

Promenade Deck
■ The First Class rooms retained their original layout and concept in their entirety.

Verandah Deck
■ The layout of this deck was completely revised. The separate facilities for Cabin and Tourist Classes were amalgamated either to serve Tourist Class in Atlantic service or to complement the facilities below on Promenade Deck whilst cruising as an open one-class vessel.
■ In one masterstroke, two lounges (Cabin on Verandah Deck and Tourist on Boat Deck) became a single two-deck space with the two levels connected with an iconic stainless steel and glass stairway. One of the largest

and most impressive rooms afloat (eventually to become the 20,000sq ft Double Room) was created. In fact, this plan had been mooted in the early design stage. Sadly, this incredible room only lasted for two years in its epic form, as the upper level mezzanine was sacrificed and severely compromised when the ship's shops were relocated there, leaving only a narrow access promenade.

■ The triplication of First, Cabin and Tourist Teenagers' Rooms was eliminated, along with the duplication of shops, bars and other smaller rooms belonging to the two lesser classes.

■ The combined Cabin and Tourist Dining Room was redesigned as a Tourist Class Restaurant.

Boat Deck

■ The layout of this was completely revised. The separate facilities for Cabin and

Tourist Classes were amalgamated either to serve Tourist Class in Atlantic service or to complement the facilities below on Promenade Deck whilst cruising as an open-class vessel.

■ Forward of the new combined double-room lounge, space formerly allocated to other Tourist facilities became the Shopping Centre (First and Tourist Classes).

■ Further forward, the original Tourist Class rooms were eliminated and replaced with a Coffee Shop, Art Gallery, Teenagers' Room and a Nightclub; all available to all passengers without any class barriers.

The most outstanding feature of these redesigned decks was their simplicity of plan, replacing the old-fashioned layouts with their numerous vestibules, galleries and other wasted circulation spaces which had no purpose.

ABOVE Only lacking the ship's name, an early publicity model of *Queen Elizabeth 2*. *(Bruce Peter Collection)*

Passenger accommodation

The design and layout of Q4's cabins did not undergo the same extensive rationalisation, except that they were no longer divided amongst three classes. The existence of mock-up cabins ensured that no real difficulties occurred because of the change in class direction.

The most expensive accommodation was arranged amidships, along the greater part of Main, Foyer and A Decks, comprising the First Class bloc on Atlantic service. However, all cabins, regardless of their category, were designed to uniformly high standards.

Gratuity policy

Even Cunard's policy on gratuities was developed with the two-class system in mind. First Class passengers were expected to pay gratuities for service whilst Tourist Class fares were all inclusive.

Trials and tribulations

Since *Queen Mary* had entered service in 1936, Cunard had introduced *Queen Elizabeth* (1940), the intermediate liner *Mauretania* (1939), the luxury cruise ship *Caronia* (1949) and post-war the combination cargo-passenger ships *Media* and *Parthia* (1946, 1947) and four cargo-passenger ships of the *Saxonia* class (1954–57). *Queen Elizabeth*, *Mauretania* and *Caronia* were outstanding ships well suited to their intended roles, but all the other ships were either outmoded before their delivery or were so shortly thereafter, being handicapped by prodigious cargo spaces that necessitated long idle periods in port whilst their cargoes were worked. The passenger fleet had been trading in the red since 1961, and by the mid-1960s *Media* and *Parthia* had been sold and two of the *Saxonia* class renamed and converted for cruising in an attempt to reverse the trend. Sir Basil seriously considered abandoning the passenger trade and selling off the incomplete Q4, concentrating instead on cargo ship operations, which were still reasonably healthy. He decided against this move, but drastic surgery was needed to turn the company around. For some years *Mauretania* had been struggling to find useful employment, her art deco interiors appearing dated when compared with modern ships in every theatre in which she was deployed. Even painting her in the company's 'cruising green' livery and sailing her between the Mediterranean and New York didn't help, and Cunard finally disposed of her for scrap towards the end of 1965. The situation was certainly grim, as the Annual Report for 1965 indicated that there had been a massive loss of £2.7 million on passenger ship services. Worse was to follow. Between May and July 1966 a seven week national seamen's strike cost the company an estimated net loss in revenue in excess of £4 million, whilst the total trading loss for the year on passenger operations was £7.5 million. It was 1966 that also saw Cunard's cargo business losing money for the first time (£0.3 million). The writing was on the wall and the moment when the surgeon should wield his knife was long overdue. By the end of 1968 *Queen Mary*, *Queen Elizabeth*, *Caronia*, *Carinthia* and *Sylvania* had all been sold and had disappeared from Cunard's sailing list. Although *Queen Elizabeth* had been given a £1.5 million makeover only two years previously and was initially earmarked to sail as the running mate to Q4 at least until 1975, annual losses of £0.75 million were deemed unsustainable, and she had to be disposed of in November 1968. John Brown Shipyard had already advised Cunard that Q4 would be delivered late, missing the summer transatlantic season with an estimated revenue loss of £200,000 per week; therefore *Queen Elizabeth* operated alone for her final season. The future Cunard passenger fleet was to comprise the new Q4 and the cruise-friendly converted *Carmania* and *Franconia*. In the event, the last two ships remained in service only until the winter of 1971, when they too were deemed uneconomic and withdrawn.

The delay in delivery of Q4 enabled Cunard to re-evaluate the class structure of the ship following a survey of 84,000 Americans. It was subsequently decided to merge the Cabin and Tourist Classes (Second and Third) into a single class. The ship would operate as a two-class ship, First and Tourist transatlantic, and as a single-class ship when cruising. The advantages of such a class structure had long been known but had previously been rejected by the management. The most significant change was that the Cabin and Third Class main lounges could now be combined into a two-deck-high lounge with a spiral staircase connecting the lower level with the mezzanine above. The room became the only two-deck-height space in the ship apart from the Theatre and was called the Double Room, with the lower level named Double Down and the upper level Double Up. Although substantially altered throughout the service life of the ship, it remained one of the defining and iconic spaces on the ship.

Launch

The ship was launched on 20 September 1967 by Her Majesty Queen Elizabeth II as *Queen Elizabeth 2 (Queen Elizabeth the Second)*, denoting with modern nomenclature that she was the second ship to be named *Queen Elizabeth*. Cunard had been negotiating with the British Government for four months for an additional loan of £3 million to complete the ship, because of increases in shipyard wages and materials which were subject to escalation clauses in the shipbuilding contract.

BELOW The two-deck-high Double Room was created by merging the former Cabin and Tourist class lounges into one. *(Bruce Peter Collection)*

LAUNCHING THE QE2

All photos Michael Gallagher Collection

RIGHT Waiting patiently for launch day.

BELOW 'I name this ship *Queen Elizabeth the Second*. May God bless her and all who sail on her.'

ABOVE Launch day royal inspection. HM the Queen talks to Lord Aberconway, Chairman of John Brown.

RIGHT *QE2* thunders into the River Clyde having been named by HM the Queen.

ABOVE LEFT *QE2* sliding down the ways.

ABOVE The stern enters the Clyde.

LEFT Alongside and fitting out at John Brown's.

Chapter Two

QE2 milestones

With the near calamity of the Q3 concept behind them, Cunard could concentrate on making sure the new Q4 would have the biggest impact on the travelling public. Whilst early engineering and outfitting issues plagued the ship's entry into service, of far greater consequence was the acquisition of Cunard by an investment group. Dogged with reliability issues, Falklands heroism, re-engining and a further take-over, *Queen Elizabeth 2* went on to become the world's most loved and most easily recognisable liner.

OPPOSITE Home Waters – celebrating Cunard's 150th anniversary. *(Gordon Bauwens)*

Completion, entry into service and Trafalgar

After countless delays and shortages, *QE2s'* three boilers were sequentially lit for the first time on 19 September 1968 for testing and the start of the dock trials which were a necessary prerequisite before taking the ship to sea. On 15 November the ship was opened to the public for viewing for the first time. The ship was far from complete but it was the first glimpse of the ship an eager public had of her interiors.

Three days later, under the command of Captain 'Bil' Warwick, *QE2* left the fitting-out berth at the shipyard where so many famous ships had been similarly completed in the past, and travelled down the River Clyde towards the sea for dry-docking, underwater cleaning and painting prior to commencement of preliminary sea trials. These began on 26 November in the Irish Sea leading up to speed trials off the Isle of Arran, and upon returning to the Clyde *Queen Elizabeth 2* was issued with a Passenger Ship Safety Certificate for the first time. Less than a month later, on 23 December, *QE2* set sail on further technical trials, during which she suffered a contaminated boiler feed and resonance in her turbines whilst sailing at high speed. Under a cloud she arrived in Southampton for the first time on 2 January 1969, and Cunard Line publicly refused to accept delivery of the ship because of the inherent machinery defects and outstanding outfit work.

After thorough theoretical analysis and testing, and with all outfitting works complete, *QE2* was finally handed over and accepted by Cunard following a successful shakedown cruise to Las Palmas, which began on 18 April 1969. The ship began her North Atlantic service on 2 May when she departed from Southampton for the first time bound for New York, arriving to a fireboat welcome five days later on 7 May. The ship then settled down to her routine of transatlantic crossings with one to two days' layover at each terminal port, punctuated with a number of pleasure cruises. In October that year Cunard announced that £2.5 million of the Government loan advanced to build the ship had been repaid, and that thereafter £500,000 would be repaid each month to clear the remaining balance of £12 million.

LEFT **Maiden arrival in Southampton.** *(Michael Gallagher Collection)*

BELOW **Maiden arrival in New York.** *(Michael Gallagher Collection)*

On 8 January 1971, whilst on a Caribbean cruise, *Queen Elizabeth 2* rescued passengers and crew from the French Line passenger ship *Antilles* which had caught fire and was in danger of sinking. Early in the year Cunard's share price began to rise when rumours circulated within the City of London about a possible take-over deal for Cunard. These rumours were confirmed when it was announced that Trafalgar House Investments had made a formal £24 million offer, and after some negotiation the Cunard Board recommended to its shareholders to accept an increased offer of £27.3 million. This was carried, and on 26 August Victor Matthews of Trafalgar House assumed the role of Chairman from Sir Basil Smallpiece.

Trafalgar lost no time in assessing the viability of Cunard and soon began to make radical changes. *QE2*'s fleetmates, *Carmania* and *Franconia*, were both withdrawn from service by October, deemed uneconomic to operate, and the focus turned to making *QE2* more of a revenue-making proposition. To this end the ship's schedule was intensified, removing the lay-over days at terminal ports, and in 1972 the ship underwent a radical £1 million refit at Vosper Thornycroft in Southampton. This entailed adding a two-deck-high block of new balcony penthouse suites in place of the semi-enclosed games area on Sports Deck and also major internal reorganisation. Later, in 1977, during a refit at Bethlehem Steel Shipyard, Bayonne, New Jersey, two further luxury suites were added forward of the earlier additions,

RIGHT **From every angle, *QE2* exhibited an exciting new look.** *(Bruce Peter Collection)*

ABOVE **The Queen Mary Suite is hoisted on board during the 1977 refit.** *(Stephen Payne Collection)*

whilst 200 miles off from Bermuda, losing all propulsion power after the boiler feed water became contaminated with oil. As it was uncertain how long repairs would take, and with the weather conditions being fine at the time, Cunard decided to transfer the 1,654 passengers to Flagship Cruises' *Sea Venture*, which was in the area. Sea Venture arrived at 3.30am on 3 April and was manoeuvred to 'dock' alongside the portside of the stricken *Queen*. Mercifully the weather remained fine and two gangways were rigged for the transfer, which took less than two hours to effect. Tugs towed *QE2* to Bermuda, where temporary repairs were effected to enable the ship to make for New York, where permanent repairs were undertaken. The ship resumed her transatlantic schedule on 16 April, sailing for Southampton.

Near disaster

On 23 July 1976 *Queen Elizabeth 2* suffered a major incident when there was an explosion and fire in the turbine room. It was only through the gallant efforts of her engineering crew that the fire was contained and put out. Five officers were subsequently awarded a commemorative plate by Mr Edmund Dell, Secretary of State for Trade, in recognition of their services during the emergency.

these being the famous Queen Mary and Queen Elizabeth Suites.

On 1 April 1974 at 4.00am in the morning the ship was involved in a major incident

RIGHT *QE2* **between 1972 and 1977, before the Queen Elizabeth and Queen Mary Suites were added behind the mast.** *(Michael Gallagher Collection)*

They were: Chief Engineer Officer Jack Marland; Deputy Chief Engineer Officer Stanley D. Child; Intermediate Second Engineer Officer Thomas A. Jackson; Fourth Engineer Officer Thomas A. Goode; and Fourth Electrical Officer John H. Griffin.

Senior Second Engineer Officer Edward R. Divett also received a letter of appreciation from Mr Dell.

The Department of Trade's citation read:

At about 04.40 hours on 23rd July, while the QE2 was on voyage from Cherbourg to New York, a turbine failure caused an oil mist explosion, which enveloped the turbine room in flames and left in its wake an oil fire that was being fed by hundreds of gallons of oil escaping from broken oil pipes.

Mr. Goode was on duty in the turbine control room when the explosion occurred, and he immediately raised the alarm. He then shut down the propulsion plant, and, realising that escaping oil was feeding the fire, he shut down the oil pumps. Although the heat and smoke were making breathing difficult, on his own initiative he then carried out numerous measures to reduce the danger.

Throughout this period, although aware that the control room was engulfed by the flames and smoke which filled the machinery space, he was not aware that unusual noises he heard around the glass-fronted control room were in fact the collapsing molten aluminium structure. When the alarm was raised Mr. Marland, Mr. Child and Mr. Griffin, wearing self-contained breathing apparatus, entered the turbine room from the boiler room, and, in conditions of intense heat and smoke, attacked with a combination of water spray and foam the main seat of the fire around the starboard turbine. In addition, Mr. Jackson entered the turbine room from the working alleyway through the aft door and tackled the fire from the other side. As a result of the combined efforts of these four men within 30 minutes the main fire had been extinguished. More fire parties were then able to enter the turbine room, and by 15.20 hours the numerous secondary fires had all been extinguished. Under Mr. Divett's leadership all the essential services were maintained throughout the emergency.

Falklands heroine

On 3 May, whilst *Queen Elizabeth 2* was sailing home from her maiden visit to the American East Coast city of Philadelphia, Her Majesty's Government led by Margaret Thatcher informed Cunard that the ship was going to be requisitioned for service in the Falklands War. The Argentinian Government, led by Lieutenant

LEFT Captain Arnott proudly looks on as Edward Divett, Stanley Child and Jack Marland receive their plaques. *(Stephen Payne Collection)*

ABOVE *QE2* is readied for the Falklands War with the helipads being fitted fore and aft. *(Bruce Peter Collection)*

General Leopoldo Galtieri, had invaded the Falkland Islands, a British Sovereign Territory located to the east of Argentina in the South Atlantic, on 2 April. The British had amassed a Naval Task Force to sail south to retake the Islands, and also that of South Georgia which had been occupied by the Argentinians. Crucial to the efforts were British troops, who would storm the Islands, and to transport them there a number of British passenger ships were requisitioned. These included P&O Cruises' venerable *Canberra* and Cunard's *Queen Elizabeth 2*. Preparations were put in hand by Vosper Thornycroft in Southampton to prefabricate two large helicopter pads, and as soon as the ship arrived in her home port work began to convert her from luxury liner to troop ship. Aft, the side windscreens on the Quarter and Upper Decks were cut away with the new helicopter pad being installed above the two aft pools with a myriad of supports. A somewhat smaller pad was fitted forward, extending towards the bow over the forecastle on Quarter Deck. Internally, some carpeted decks were covered with sheets of plywood for protection and bulkheads were also temporarily sheathed to protect them. Some of the carpet on 'D' Stairway midships was taken up and stored, thereby exposing the steel deck. Arrangements were made for refuelling at sea (RAS) whilst under way, with temporary pipework being installed from the starboard side midships baggage shell door on Two Deck to the fuel tanks some six decks below. Additional fresh water generation capacity was added by installing a reverse osmosis unit, and a secure military communications room was also installed behind the bridge. With the ship secured alongside, during a five-day period large numbers of artworks were removed from the ship for safe keeping ashore. On 12 May troop embarkation commenced at 5.45am, and by mid-afternoon approximately 3,000 men had walked up the gangway and were finding their way around the ship. Of over 1,000 crew who volunteered for the voyage, about 650 were chosen by Cunard to man the ship.

With troops embarked, *Queen Elizabeth 2* prepared to sail south. However, there were serious concerns about her propulsion plant, notably the boilers. All three would be required to provide sufficient steam for a fast passage but only one was immediately serviceable. It was crucial for the ship to sail from Southampton as previously announced, as representatives of the world's media would be on hand and the news of the departure would send a clear signal to Argentina that Great Britain meant business. At the appointed time, 4.03pm to be precise, *Queen Elizabeth 2* eased away from the Queen Elizabeth II Terminal in the Eastern Docks with the aid of tugs. Families and friends of the embarked troops and a large crowd of the general public waved the ship off, accompanied by the stirring music of a military band. With many others I was at the end of Hythe Pier, which the ship would pass as she headed up the Solent to Southampton Water and the open sea beyond. The ship sailed with her single boiler, but once out at sea in the western approaches she was manoeuvred into an area outside normal shipping lanes and discreetly anchored whilst work proceeded to mend the defective boilers. Following repairs, she headed south for Freetown, Sierra Leone, where she arrived at 9.00am on 18 May. During this initial passage she practised refuelling at sea. The troops exercised by jogging around the Boat Deck and engaged in numerous weapons drills to hone their ability to effectively wage war against the aggressors. At Freetown the ship took on fuel and fresh water before sailing later that day for Ascension Island, where additional ordnance was airlifted on board whilst she lay at anchor after arriving on the 20th. Three days later the ship left Ascension and sailed for South Georgia, which had been quickly recaptured by the British. The ship sailed with extra lookouts but not radar, as this could have given her position away to the enemy or to others, and surprise was a key element of any future military action. As *Queen Elizabeth 2* approached the war zone, she began zig-zagging (frequently altering course to make targeting difficult, whilst still maintaining a set course overall), as the earlier *Queens* had done during the Second World War.

The ship arrived at South Georgia on 27 May shortly after 6.00pm amid thick winter fog with zero visibility and zero prospect of offloading her troops. *QE2* anchored in Cumberland Bay East with other units of the mercantile Task Force, including *Canberra* and the ferry *Norland*. Shortly before midnight the first troop transfers began, with 700 men being moved to the other ships. Transfers continued until the following evening, using launches, helicopters and tugs, until all the troops had safely embarked for the second part of their journey. On 29 May 640 survivors from three Royal Navy ships sunk by the Argentinians, *Ardent*, *Coventry* and *Antelope*, embarked for the journey home to the United Kingdom. On 11 June *Queen Elizabeth 2* arrived back in the Solent, where the personnel on board received a hero's welcome. Admiral Sir John Fieldhouse, Commander-in-Chief of the Falklands operation, arrived on board by helicopter with the Cunard Chairman Lord Victor Matthews, and both men addressed the troops and the liner's brave crew. Proceeding towards Southampton Water, the Royal Yacht

Britannia with Her Majesty Queen Elizabeth the Queen Mother on board sailed in convoy with the *Queen Elizabeth 2* to salute all. All those on board the Cunard flagship gave three great cheers to Her Majesty.

Her Majesty the Queen Mother sent Captain Peter Jackson the following message:

> I am pleased to welcome you back as *QE2* returns to home waters after your tour of duty in the South Atlantic. The exploits of your own ship's company and the deeds of valour of those who served Antelope, Coventry and Ardent have been acclaimed throughout the land and I am proud to add my personal tribute.

To which Captain Jackson replied:

> Please convey to Her Majesty Queen Elizabeth our thanks for her kind message. Cunard's *Queen Elizabeth 2* is proud to have been of service to Her Majesty's forces.

These two messages were transferred to a silver plaque and formed part of the Heritage Trail that was subsequently installed on board the ship. *Queen Elizabeth 2* had sailed 14,967 miles in less than a month. She was subsequently refitted by Vosper Thornycroft and, following 24 hours of engine trials at sea on 7 August after two months of refitting, she returned to commercial service.

The refit was substantially paid for by HM Government, but the public purse was

ABOVE Sporting a pebble-grey hull and Cunard funnel colours, QE2 enters New York on her first post-Falklands visit. *(Michael Gallagher Collection)*

only opened to return the ship to the same condition she was in when requisitioned. This entailed reinstating the aft deck configuration by removing the helicopter platform, and similarly removing the forward pad. Cunard chose wisely to extend the extent of the refit and also instigated two major livery changes. First, the charcoal-grey dark hull was replaced by light

RIGHT Post-Falklands refit engine trials 1982. *(Michael Gallagher Collection)*

pebble-grey; a move that was reversed in June 1983 when it became apparent how difficult it was to keep looking pristine. The second major change was permanent. The main body of the slim funnel uptake, hitherto painted white against Cunard's previous heritage, was repainted in vibrant Cunard red with slim black bands.

Carnival and Istithmar

In 1995 Trafalgar House was taken over by the Anglo-Norwegian Kvaerner Group, primarily to obtain the construction company Cementation. Kvaerner was not interested in Cunard and immediately put the company up for sale. Following an upsurge in transatlantic bookings, stemming from the success of James Cameron's movie *Titanic*, Cunard was purchased by Carnival Corporation in May 1998; and within two years an order had been placed for a new transatlantic liner, to be named *Queen Mary 2*.

In 2004 Cunard's new transatlantic liner *Queen Mary 2* entered service. At nearly 150,000grt she was more than twice the size of *Queen Elizabeth 2*, and the new ship marked a new era in transatlantic travel. Festooned with the modern prerequisite of the balcony, she offered a wide range of accommodation with many spectacular public spaces, in an attempt to recapture the spirit of the 'Great Ships of State' of the 1930s. *Queen Mary 2* spent her first few months of Cunard service cruising the Caribbean after a tumultuous maiden voyage to Fort Lauderdale. She eventually sailed on her first transatlantic crossing on 16 April. Despite encountering a particularly severe North Atlantic storm, she managed to reach New York on schedule. There she was joined by *Queen Elizabeth 2*, which looked decidedly diminutive alongside her younger sibling. The two ships sailed in tandem back across the Atlantic. During a ceremony on 1 May at Southampton, *Queen Elizabeth 2* formally relinquished her role as flagship of Cunard Line through the transfer of the symbolic 'Britannia' cup to *Queen Mary 2* by one of the latter's tenders. The *Britannia* cup, also known as the Boston cup, is a large solid silver cup, that was presented to Cunard by the citizens of the American city of Boston as

thanks to Cunard for choosing Boston as the American terminus for its fledgling transatlantic service. *Queen Elizabeth 2* then became a successful full-time cruise ship, sailing primarily to the Norwegian fjords, the Mediterranean and the Canary Islands, as well as making an extended three-month annual World Cruise.

On 18 June 2007 Cunard stunned the cruise community by announcing that the sale of *Queen Elizabeth 2* to Istithmar/Nakheel, part of the Dubai World group of companies, had been agreed, for US$100 million. The intention was that the ship, once delivered to Dubai, would be converted into a floating hotel and resort and moored within a newly created island complex off Dubai called the Palm Jumeirah.

WORLD CRUISING

ABOVE *QE2* prepares to put to sea from Southampton on her 2006 World Cruise. *(Stephen Payne Collection)*

RIGHT *QE2* in the Panama Canal. *(Michael Gallagher Collection)*

RIGHT *QE2* at Pier 90, Berth 3 (Manhattan, New York) with Royal Caribbean's *Nordic Prince*. *(Michael Gallagher Collection)*

TOP Final US farewell.
*(Michael Gallagher
Collection)*

ABOVE *QE2* makes a
fine sight as she edges
away from the Queen
Elizabeth II Terminal on
her penultimate cruise
to the Mediterranean.
*(Stephen Payne
Collection)*

LEFT *QE2* at Cape
Town in the mid-1980s.
(Bruce Peter Collection)

ABOVE *QE2* within Panama Canal's Gaillard Cut during a post re-engining World Cruise in 2006. *(Michael Gallagher Collection)*

It was assumed that new international safety regulations passed by the International Maritime Organisation affecting passenger ships from June 2010 had forced the ship into retirement, as the costs of the necessary upgrades would have been very onerous. However, some sources believe that Britain's Maritime Coast Guard Agency (MCA) had already sanctioned that *QE2* could have remained in service with minimal alterations.

The ship's final season included the inevitable final visits to ports around the world where the ship had been a familiar albeit temporary backdrop for nearly four decades. Particularly poignant was the last World Cruise, where, in tandem with *Queen Mary 2*, Sydney was brought to a virtual standstill as sightseers flocked to get one more final glimpse of the great liner. Then there was a cruise around the British Isles, where the ship was feted at

BELOW Her Majesty Queen Elizabeth II with former masters of the *QE2* during her visit to the ship in Southampton on 2 June 2008. Back, left to right: Capt Keith Stanley, Capt Robert Arnott, Capt Robin Woodall, Capt Nicholas Bates, Capt Ray Heath, Capt Lawrence Portet, Capt Peter Jackson and Capt Roland Hasell. Front: Commodore John Burton-Hall, Capt Ian McNaught, HM Queen Elizabeth II, Capt David Perkins and Commodore Warwick. *(Arthur Edwards/AFP/Getty Images)*

RIGHT HM the Queen unveiled a painting of the *QE2* passing through Southampton Water by Isle of Wight artist Robert Lloyd during her visit to the *QE2* in Southampton on 2 June 2008. The Queen bade a fond farewell to the liner that bore her name before it sailed off for a new life as a floating hotel in Dubai. *(Arthur Edwards/AFP/Getty Images)*

each port of call, crowds flocking to see the ship wherever she went. On 30 September she embarked on her Farewell to Britain cruise, with calls at Cobh, Dublin, Liverpool, Belfast, Glasgow, Edinburgh and Newcastle before returning to Southampton on 10 October. The day she visited her birthplace on the Clyde, 5 October, she was accompanied by wonderful weather, and the ship made a fine sight on the Clyde in company with HMS *Ark Royal* and other Royal Navy ships. On 10 October, in tandem with *Queen Mary 2*, she set off on her final round trip of the Atlantic, arriving in New York on 16 October. It was *Queen Elizabeth 2*'s 710th visit to the port, and she was berthed at the traditional Manhattan piers. Sailing back to Southampton again that afternoon, she backed out into the Hudson before moving

down the river to join *Queen Mary 2*, which was waiting for her having sailed from the new Cunard New York terminal at Brooklyn. The two great Cunarders motored past the Statue of Liberty as dusk descended before sailing under the Verrazano Narrows Bridge, creating a magnificent spectacle. Sailing in tandem, the two ships crossed the North Atlantic before a final gesture on the last day at sea, when *Queen Mary 2* staged a close sail past on *QE2*'s starboard side before speeding off to allow an earlier Southampton arrival, on 22 October. The atmosphere on board *QE2* had been electric throughout the voyage,

BELOW *QE2* swings in the Clyde on her last visit, 5 October 2008. *(Gordon Bauwens Collection)*

LEFT Two mighty *Queens*. *(Michael Gallagher Collection)*

CENTRE The final transatlantic voyage in the company of *Queen Mary 2*. *(Michael Gallagher Collection)*

BOTTOM Keeping station with *Queen Mary 2*. *(Stephen Payne Collection)*

for although it was tinged with sadness, everybody wanted to make the most of the ship's final trip across the pond. Throughout, the ship was flying a bright red 'Paying Off' pennant from the masthead.

The penultimate cruise sailing, on 27 October, was an extended cruise through the Mediterranean, venturing as far afield as Piraeus, Athens. This cruise, like all of the 'Farewell Season' voyages, was a complete sell-out, testament to the love and affection of the travelling public who were eager for one last gasp of nostalgia.

The last voyage

The sale contract stipulated that the ship had to be delivered to Dubai in a complete in-service condition, with nothing removed. The final voyage was due to leave Southampton on 11 November. On the approach to Southampton at 5.26am, off the Brambles Bank near Calshot, *QE2* ran aground just as *Queen Elizabeth* had done on 17 April 1947. Luckily, the ship was refloated by 6.10am and with the aid of several tugs she was subsequently safely moored at the Queen Elizabeth II Terminal, with her bow pointing up the Solent and towards the open sea. Divers were sent down to inspect the hull and they found nothing untoward, the ship having been undamaged by the incident. During the day a Farewell Reception was held on board attended by His Royal Highness Prince Philip. The royal visitor took particular interest in the ship and made an extensive tour, talking to crew members, past and present, wherever he went. Southampton prepared to pay homage to the great ship, and a large flotilla of pleasure craft and the preserved steamer *Shieldhall* gathered in the area to see the ship off. As it was early November, dusk had given way to darkness by 7.15pm as *QE2* eased away from her berth, with fireworks punctuating the night sky. *Queen Elizabeth 2* majestically set sail in convoy with the multitude of pleasure craft and the *Shieldhall* – on which I was aboard with my family, down the Solent to the cacophony of sirens and whistles, not least *QE2's* own powerful Typhon whistles. Within an hour she had safely navigated Southampton Water and around the Brambles Bank into the Solent, making a left-hand turn shortly thereafter to pass Cowes and Ryde on the Isle of Wight before turning south towards the English Channel. After spending 12 November traversing the Bay of Biscay, on 13 November she arrived at Lisbon. The ship then sailed through the Strait of Gibraltar, stopping off at the famous Rock on the 14th, before entering the Mediterranean for the final time and heading to Civitavecchia for Rome on the 16th, Naples on the 17th and Valletta, Malta, on the 18th. A further stop was made at Alexandria on the 20th before she transited the Suez Canal on the 22nd. Thereafter she was at sea until she approached Dubai.

QE2 made her final landfall and docked at Port Rashid, Dubai, on 26 November. She was greeted at the entrance to Dubai by a flotilla of 120 smaller vessels, very much like the welcome *Queen Mary* had received when she arrived at Long Beach for her retirement in November 1967. The following day, with her last passengers still on board, *QE2* was officially signed over to her new owners at 1405hrs on 27 November 2008, with the Cunard President Carol Marlow and her last Master Captain Ian McNaught officiating at the ceremony. The hand-over complete, the crew disembarked, the passengers having left the previous day. The ship was then moved to the commercial cargo port to allow the passenger terminal to be used by visiting cruise ships. Cunard had ensured that the ship couldn't be used for any other purpose other than the hotel project at Dubai by the inclusion of a covenant in the sale contract. This gave Cunard the right to veto any alternative use or location until 2018, a full ten years after her sale. Nakheel, the new owners, had previously released details of their plans. These entailed largely gutting the passenger cabin areas and installing new luxury cabins. Some of the public rooms were to be refurbished in their original configuration whilst others were to be replaced, changing their functions. The existing funnel was to be taken ashore, to be replaced by a glass-fronted facsimile that would house the hotel's most expensive suites, whilst the ship's Heritage Trail would be showcased in an adjacent museum.

In the event, the financial crash that had unfolded throughout 2008 had a profound

BELOW Embarking passengers for the last voyage to Dubai, 11 November 2008. *(Stephen Payne Collection)*

effect on these grandiose plans. The plain fact was that as *Queen Elizabeth 2* tied up at her Dubai berth there was simply no money available to refit her. The ship was initially cared for by a team of engineers from the ship management company V Ships, who kept the machinery maintained. They were joined for a short period by the ship's former Master, Captain Ronald Warwick, who was employed to ensure the safety of the ship, his detailed knowledge of *QE2* being deemed an essential contribution to the care and maintenance team. All plans for the refit were quietly dropped, and the ship remained in limbo at Dubai with her red Cunard titles painted over and her port of registry changed from Southampton to Port Vila, Vanuatu.

In July 2009 Nakheel announced that the ship was to transfer to Cape Town, in South Africa, to become a floating hotel there. Cunard were required to give their consent, which they did conditional on receipt of various heritage Cunard items. These included a famous silver model of *Queen Elizabeth 2*, commissioned by Trafalgar House, that was displayed within the Midships Lobby during the ship's latter sailing days. The bust of HM the Queen which adorned the Queens Room was also acquired,

and both these items now feature on board the present Cunard *Queen Elizabeth*. However, despite initial optimism the transfer to South Africa never took place, and the *QE2* remained at Dubai. Rumours and speculation about her future continued unabated, but any suggestion that the ship would be scrapped were firmly repudiated by her owners. On 28 January 2011 *QE2* broke free from her moorings during a particularly bad storm and was set adrift in the harbour. Luckily she was retrieved unharmed from her unintentional excursion and docked once again at Port Rashid. Later that year, on 21 March, *QE2* was able to exchange whistle salutes with *Queen Mary 2*, as the ship was still manned and maintained by her professional crew. At the end of the year she was opened to host a sumptuous New Year's Eve Party for 1,000 guests, being managed for the black tie event by Global Event Management.

On 2 July 2012 it was announced that the ship would open as a 300-bedroom hotel after an 18-month refit, which would largely restore the ship to her delivered condition complete with Heritage Trail. The intention was to moor the ship alongside the Port Rashid Cruise Terminal, which was to be similarly refurbished and to include a special maritime museum. Sadly, this optimism was unfounded as the ship remained laid up without any significant work being undertaken, although at one stage she did spend some time in a local dry dock. Further rumours circulated, including speculation that she would be scrapped in China, whilst various other bids for her were forthcoming, including the *QE2* London project. This latter was promulgated by John Chillingworth, one of the ship's former engineers, and included a £20 million acquisition and a £40 million refurbishment. The plan called for the ship to be moored on the Thames opposite the O2 Arena, and it was claimed the enterprise would support 2,000 jobs and had the support of the then Mayor of London, Boris Johnson. An alternative plan announced in January 2013 would have seen the ship becoming a floating hotel and resort in Asia, but like all previous plans this appears to have been abandoned.

At the time of writing, in July 2016, *Queen Elizabeth 2* continues her solitary existence in

BELOW *Queen Elizabeth 2* **moored at Dubai.** *(Michael Gallagher Collection)*

QE2: THE TRIUMPH OF A GREAT TRADITION

FAREWELL
CELEBRATION
2008

Queen Elizabeth 2

CUNARD

DINNER ON BOARD
QUEEN ELIZABETH 2
WEDNESDAY 26 NOVEMBER 2008

THE MOST FAMOUS OCEAN LINERS IN THE WORLD™

LEFT The last dinner.
(Stephen Payne Collection)

Dubai, being moved around the dock complex from time to time. It is reported that the extensive care and maintenance crew has been drastically reduced to little more than a watch-keeping contingent, and that she is to all intents and purposes a dead ship. What the future holds is unknown, but whatever eventually happens to this remarkable ship, her legacy and influence on the maritime scene will live on forever.

BELOW *QE2* **quietly rests in Dubai as** *Queen Elizabeth* **approaches the port.**
(Michael Gallagher Collection)

Chapter Three

Anatomy of *Queen Elizabeth 2*

The design of *Queen Elizabeth 2* would break with all traditions of what went where and how it was made. Prefabrication, lighter materials and a styling job that would mark the ship out to be something completely fresh and exciting were the orders of the day. Cunard would never be the same again.

OPPOSITE Almost ready for launching. *(Michael Gallagher Collection)*

The design of Q4

Q4 had its origins in the lessons learned from Q3. Cunard's technical team, led by naval architect Dan Wallace and marine engineer Tom Kameen, was convinced that a ship of some 58,000 tons, driven by two screws rather than four, could do the job of the original ship of 75,000grt.

Unlike the earlier *Queens* and Q3, Q4 would be able to pass through the Panama Canal if required on extended voyages. In fact, Dan Wallace had visited the Panama Canal during October 1961 to obtain such an agreement for transits. Significantly, the 29.5kt weekly Atlantic service would be achieved with much less power than Q3. As a three-class vessel Q4 would be a very flexible unit, with blurred class demarcations allowing groups of cabins to be allocated to two classes as demand suggested. Thus First Class would range from 300 to 500 passengers; Cabin Class from 526 to 600 and Tourist Class from 770 to 954.

Cunard planned to engage the best outside designers, not only for the passenger accommodation but also for the exterior profile, to ensure the ship was attractive and forward looking in every way. James Gardner was appointed as Joint Design Coordinator, with particular emphasis being placed on the exterior look of the ship. Gardner was a well-known designer who had been instrumental in creating the dummy inflatable tanks that were used to mislead German military planners during the Second World War, as well as the public decorations commissioned for Queen Elizabeth II's Coronation.

Gardner particularly disliked the 'form' of ships' funnels and was determined to perfect something different for *QE2*. A ship's funnel has two main functions. First, and most obviously, it has to be so designed that the smoke, soot and smuts from the main machinery installation are discharged in such a way that under almost all operating conditions the offending efflux falls away from the ship and thus does not contaminate the decks or get sucked into the air-conditioning and other intakes. This can be difficult to achieve, as a funnel structure invariably produces a low-pressure area directly behind itself as a consequence of the airflow around it. Traditionally, wind tunnel tests with scale models and wind speeds at scale speed were used to perfect designs, but these days the practice relies more heavily on computer modelling. Secondly, a funnel acts as a giant billboard displaying the company's colours, so that the ship's ownership is instantly recognised. Gardner devised a thin tall structure that minimised the incongruous low-pressure effect and cleverly

RIGHT Tom Kameen, Cunard's Technical Director. *(Michael Gallagher Collection)*

FAR RIGHT James Gardner was the QE2's inspirational external stylist. *(Bruce Peter Collection)*

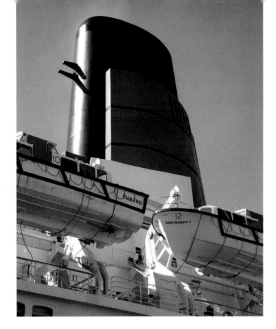

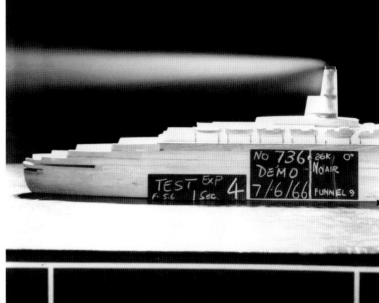

ABOVE **Gardner's thin, tall funnel.**
(Michael Gallagher Collection)

ABOVE RIGHT **Q4 wind tunnel funnel optimisation tests at NPL.** *(Bruce Peter Collection)*

RIGHT **Passing beneath the Tagus river bridge in Lisbon was a tight fit.** *(Blair Skilton)*

directed the exhaust ventilation air from the engine room to fill in what was remaining. As for the company's funnel colours of Cunard red and black, these were redistributed on the funnel in a most intriguing manner. The central core of the funnel was painted black from top to bottom, but side curtain surfaces eschewed the normal Cunard red (at least until 1982) and were painted white. A new device, a shallow wind scoop that caught and directed the forward to aft airflow that gave the smuts a gentle skywards boost, was internally painted Cunard red. So all the traditional colours were present, but not where they were expected.

Gardner also played with the upper superstructure, painting the Boat Deck longitudinal bulkhead khaki instead of white. The idea was to create a darker region in shadow that would make it appear that the lifeboats and tenders were hovering in mid-air, the illusion being compounded by painting the lifeboat davits black, instead of white. The

RIGHT **A detail view of the bridge and superstructure front.** *(Stephen Payne Collection)*

forward-facing end of the Sports Deck was similarly treated to make it look as though the bridge was floating above the ship. The single mast set behind the bridge didn't escape unscathed either, its lower part being painted black. The demarcation between hull and superstructure and its paint treatment was also deemed important by Gardner, and he set the separation at Two Deck level, softening the approach by substituting charcoal-grey for black. The white waterline stripe and the red boot topping were traditional. At the aft end of the funnel house on Signal Deck was painted the ship's name, *Queen Elizabeth 2*, ingeniously positioned where passengers on the aft Sports Deck could have their photographs taken with the ship name in the background – long before the ubiquitous selfie came into fashion.

Q4 would be built in the traditional manner on an inclined slipway by laying a keel and double bottom structure before building up the rest of the ship. Although prefabricated blocks and sections would be used, these were very modest in size compared to today's practice. It was estimated that it would take about four years to build Q4, giving an approximate delivery date towards the end of 1966, allowing for the continuing development of the design. Delivery in the spring of the year was no longer deemed important as Q4 was designed for cruising as much as for the North Atlantic service, and she could slot into service at any time of the year.

Most importantly, the concept of Q4 departed radically from that of the previous *Queens* and Q3 in three ways:

- ■ The ability to cruise successfully worldwide
- ■ Higher flexibility between the classes, with all en suite facility accommodation
- ■ Greatly reduced operating costs through hydrodynamic advances and rapid progress in marine engineering design.

In May 1964 two important decisions were announced: that the ship would carry three classes of passenger and, in a total break with convention, would have three restaurants located above the main passenger deck rather than, as was traditional, low down in the ship. All cabins were to be fitted with baths or showers and toilets.

At the same time secret tests were being carried out at the Ship Research Laboratory on a 22ft-long wax model of the hull of the

proposed new ship. The most significant development from these tests was the provision of a slightly bulbous bow to reduce pitching in rough seas. The model had already been tried in the 1,300ft-long tank at Feltham, the longest of its kind in the world.

The new Cunarder would be 960ft in length with a draught of 31ft; gross tonnage about 58,000; and her twin-screw turbine machinery would be capable of developing a maximum of 110,000hp. Service speed would be 28½kt on less than half the fuel consumption of a 'Queen'. Again, the machinery weight would only be one-third that of a 'Queen' liner and the engine room complement considerably less than half. The ship would carry as many passengers as a 'Queen'. Uncluttered upper decks with two large swimming pools, lido areas which were to be the largest afloat, a hitherto unequalled use of large glass windows in promenade decks, side screens, passengers' cabins and in the restaurants would contribute to the ship's modern appearance; and the extensive use of glass would mean a maximum amount of natural daylight. For instance, 1,400 passengers would be accommodated in cabins with portholes. Again, recognising that passengers expected continuing improvement in the standards of cabin comfort, Cunard gave a lot of thought to fitting the greatest possible number of beds rather than upper berths. Of a total passenger capacity of 2,050, all of whom were to be accommodated in rooms matching the highest standards of competitive ships, only 10% would occupy upper berths.

It was these features which were essential to North Atlantic service as well as cruising.

Great emphasis was placed on ensuring that Q4 could be used as a dual-purpose ship, and Cunard promulgated the notion that the ship would be the first to embrace duality. This wasn't in fact the case, as Canadian Pacific's celebrated *Empress of Britain* (1931; 42,348grt) had sailed pre-war on the Atlantic using four screws in summer, switching to cruising on two screws in the winter; and Cunard's own *Caronia* (1949; 34,183grt) was considered a dual-purpose ship, which deputised for the *Queens* on the Atlantic when they were undergoing their biannual maintenance periods, and otherwise cruised around the world. However, both *Empress of*

ABOVE The Caronia Restaurant was once the Columbia. *(Stephen Payne Collection)*

LEFT The bulbous bow. *(Michael Gallagher Collection)*

BELOW Uncluttered simplicity of form characterised *QE2*'s original design. *(Bruce Peter Collection)*

1 Lido decks with open air
   swimming pools (x 2)
2 Q4 Room
3 Double Room
4 Queen's Room
5 Safety Control Room
6 Shops
7 Funnel
8 Kennels
9 Lifeboats (x 20)
10 Theatre Bar
11 Columbia Restaurant
12 Children's Room
13 Theatre
14 Coffee Shop
15 Britannia Restaurant
16 Kitchens
17 Mast
18 Bridge and Chartroom
19 5-ton deck cranes (x 2)
20 Forecastle and anchor
   machinery
21 Bow
22 Bulb
23 Bow anchors (x 3)
24 Forward mooring deck
25 1,000hp bow thrusters (x 2)
26 Passenger accommodation
27 Printing shop
28 Hospital
29 Midships lobby
30 Turbo-alternator Room
31 Boiler Room
32 Stabilisers
33 Engine Room
34 Indoor swimming pool and
   Turkish baths
35 Laundry
36 Passenger accommodation
37 Revolving car lift
38 Launderettes (x 3)
39 Six-bladed 19ft-diameter
   31-ton propellers (x 2)
40 Crew accommodation
41 Semi-balanced rudder
42 Aft mooring deck
43 Stern

Britain and *Caronia* were much smaller and slower than the ship Cunard was contemplating.

In 1963 the company approached the Government for a loan to assist with the construction of Q4, the previous workings in relation to Q3 being redundant. It was anticipated that the ship would cost £22 million, and Cunard requested a loan of £18 million with repayments over 25 years at 4.5% interest. The Government refused these terms and rejected the supposition that the vessel was a special case. Instead it directed Cunard to explore an existing arrangement that was open to ship owners, namely the Shipbuilding Credit Scheme, which had interest payments fixed at 4.875%. However, after further negotiations, Sir John Brocklebank announced on 21 October that the Government had agreed to provide a maximum of £17.6 million at 4.5% interest on delivery of the ship. At this time the three-class structure of the ship persisted, despite misgivings by many and the clear advantages of adopting a two-class orientation.

It was intended that the new ship, being a replacement for *Queen Mary*, would run in tandem with *Queen Elizabeth* for an extended period before that ship was ultimately replaced by a new ship following evaluation of Q4's performance. To that end it was decided to substantially upgrade *Queen Elizabeth* over a four month £1.5 million refit to make her a more suitable running mate. Cunard had consistently held the view that the *Queens* were not suited to cruising because of their deep draughts, limited fresh water capacity and lack of air-conditioning and laundry facilities. Even with the virtual collapse of the winter transatlantic trade, the ships continued to cross the Atlantic, sometimes with more crew than passengers on board. Inexplicably, the ships were dry-docked twice a year for maintenance, including a spell during the profitable summer season when they should have been earning revenue.

Queen Elizabeth's refit was undertaken at Greenock on the Clyde by John Brown. It extended the air-conditioning system to cover the whole ship, a sea-water distillation plant was installed to augment fresh water tankage and therefore to extend the range of the ship,

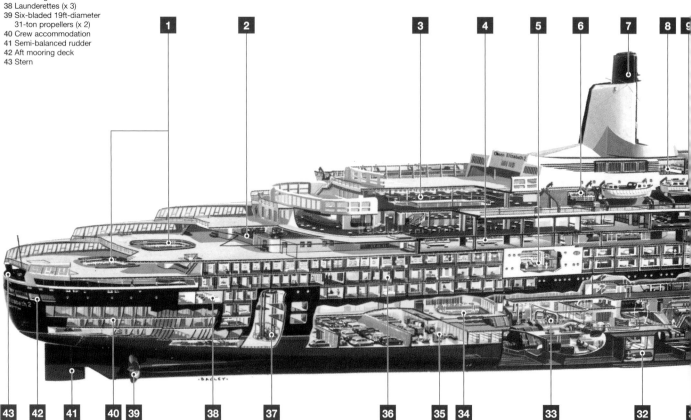

some public rooms were redecorated, some cabins were upgraded with the installation of private facilities and some were redecorated, and a new lido was built aft by extending the Promenade Deck slightly beyond the existing docking bridge and incorporating a large swimming pool and side screens. Two pairs of stabilisers had already been squeezed into the machinery spaces during two refits in 1954/55, which had greatly improved the habitability of the ship in rough weather. Whilst many of the changes were judged positively, some of the redecorated areas were completely out of place on the ship. During the same period, *Saxonia* and *Ivernia*, two of Cunard's Canadian service quartet, were renamed *Carmania* and *Franconia* respectively and similarly rebuilt with cruise service in mind. The two ships were seen as something of a test bed for new ideas that if successful could be incorporated into Q4. On the structural side, a perforated structural web was employed, which was to feature heavily in the design of Q4. This enabled 'tween-deck heights to be minimised by routing cabling and pipework through the perforations.

Styling for *Queen Elizabeth 2*

Queen Elizabeth 2 was designed from the outset to be a flexible ship, sailing on the transatlantic route between Southampton and New York on a five-day schedule at a sustained speed of 28.5kt for nine months of the year and to spend three months engaged upon more leisurely cruising. She was specifically dimensioned so that she could traverse the original Panama Canal, her 105ft breadth and 963ft length just squeezing into the Panama locks. With her draught restricted to 32ft 6in, she could sail independently of the tides at Southampton and New York, unlike the earlier *Queens* that had to time their arrivals and departures for high water.

The ship was so different from everything that had gone before. Polished woods and veneers gave way to plastic and Formica, whilst polished brass gave way to polished chrome. All the cabins throughout the classes were air-conditioned and all had private en suite facilities. Originally anticipated to have had a gross tonnage of 58,000, where 1grt represented 100cu ft of space (not a weight measurement),

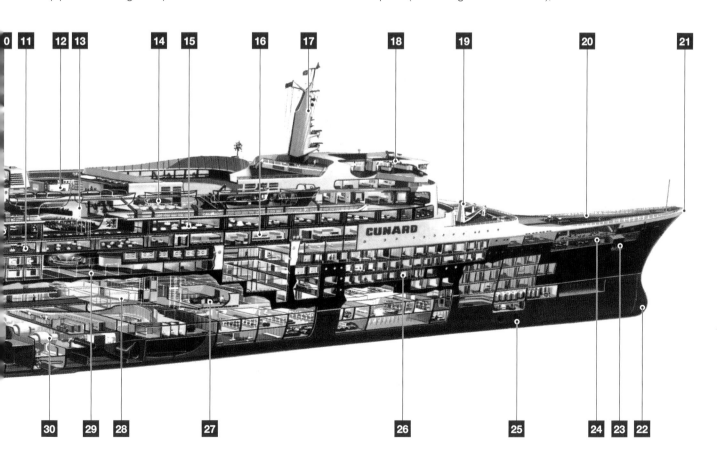

ABOVE *QE2* enters the Panama Canal. *(Michael Gallagher Collection)*

RIGHT AND FAR RIGHT Forward draught marks, draught 32ft (left) and aft draught marks (32.5ft). The difference between the forward and aft marks gives the vessel's trim, which in this case is 0.5ft by the stern. If the forward mark is deeper than the aft mark, the ship will become difficult to steer and will lose propulsion efficiency. *(Tony Skilton)*

the ship was finally measured at 65,000grt when she entered service in 1969. Despite this, she accommodated more passengers than either of the previous *Queens* and provided each passenger with 72sq ft of passenger space compared to 47.75sq ft on the old *Queen Elizabeth*.

Cunard's naval architect, Dan Wallace, led the project and worked in close co-operation with Cunard's Director of Engineering Tom Kameen and John Brown Shipyard's Technical Director and Naval Architect John Starks. In order to give the ship a unique and innovative exterior form, the architect James Gardner was appointed to oversee superstructure styling and Dennis Lennon the interior design co-ordination.

Passenger accommodation

As designed, the passenger accommodation was arranged on five decks, the greatest care having been taken to ensure the maximum number of outside rooms. At the time experience indicated that even with air-conditioning, passengers had a strong preference for rooms with natural daylight, and that many passengers would refuse to sail in an inside room. Five decades later, passengers are even more demanding, and the desirability of window cabins has been usurped by balcony cabins. On *Queen Elizabeth 2* about 75% of the passenger count occupied outside rooms. To suit modern demands there was also a very considerable emphasis on the provision of two-berth cabins. A few four-berth cabins were provided, mainly for students or families who wished to travel at minimum rate. At the time it was also identified that there would be an ever-increasing demand for families to occupy adjoining rooms, and a large number of communicating doors were therefore fitted. Many of the outer rooms were linked to an inner room by a communicating door. This allowed the inner cabin to be used by children, or when cruising it could be used as an additional dressing-room and luggage store if purchased in combination with the outer cabin.

All passenger cabins were provided with a private WC and bath or shower. Great efforts were also made to supply large wardrobes or trunk spaces and a maximum number of drawers, these latter facilities being deemed

LEFT The designer of much of *QE2*'s original interiors, Dennis Lennon. *(Bruce Peter Collection)*

BELOW The tiered aft decks as shown on the builders' model. *(Stephen Payne Collection)*

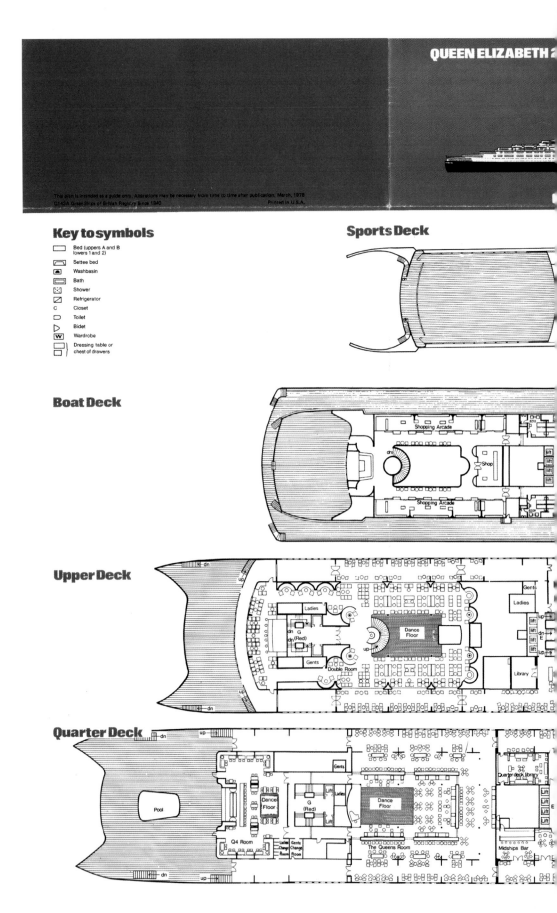

QUEEN ELIZABETH 2

This plan is intended as a guide only. Alterations may be necessary from time to time after publication. March, 1978
Q143A Great Ships of British Registry Since 1840   Printed in U.S.A.

Key to symbols

▭	Bed (uppers A and B lowers 1 and 2)
▱	Settee bed
▣	Washbasin
▭	Bath
⊠	Shower
⊿	Refrigerator
C	Closet
▭	Toilet
▷	Bidet
W	Wardrobe
▭	Dressing table or chest of drawers

Sports Deck

Boat Deck

Upper Deck

Quarter Deck

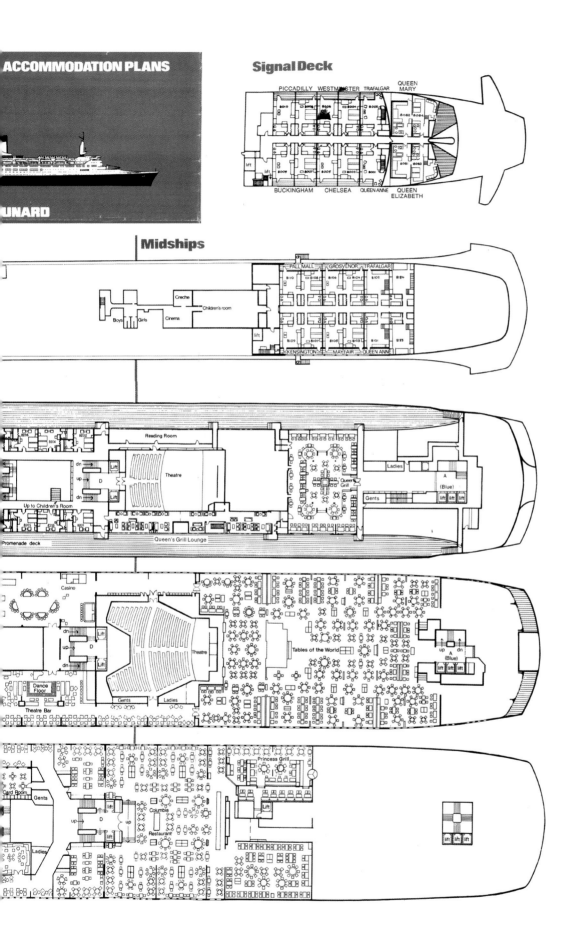

ACCOMMODATION PLANS

CUNARD

Signal Deck

PICCADILLY WESTMINSTER TRAFALGAR QUEEN MARY

BUCKINGHAM   CHELSEA   QUEEN ANNE   QUEEN ELIZABETH

Midships

PALL MALL   GROSVENOR   TRAFALGAR

KENSINGTON   MAYFAIR   QUEEN ANNE

Creche
Children's room
Boys   Girls   Cinema

Reading Room

Theatre

Queen Grill

Ladies

A
(Blue)

Gents

Up to Children's Room

Promenade deck

Queen's Grill Lounge

Casino

Theatre

Tables of the World

Dance Floor

Theatre Bar

Gents   Ladies

A
(Blue)

Card Room   Gents

Columbia Restaurant

Ladies

Princess Grill

Lift

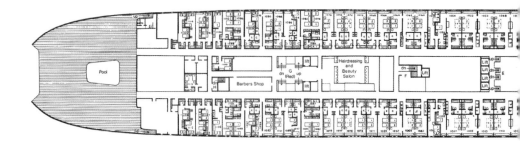

Key to symbols

▭	Bed (uppers A and B lowers 1 and 2)
◠	Settee bed
◼	Washbasin
▭	Bath
⊡	Shower
◪	Refrigerator
C	Closet
▭	Toilet
▷	Bidet
W	Wardrobe
▭	Dressing table or chest of drawers

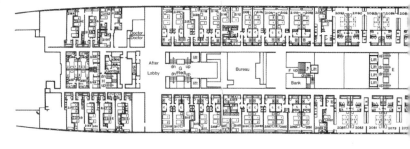

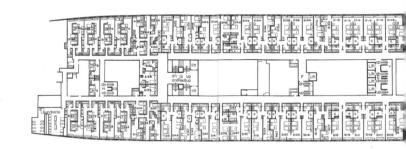

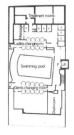

Six Deck

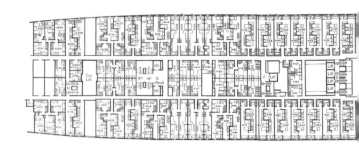

Seven Deck

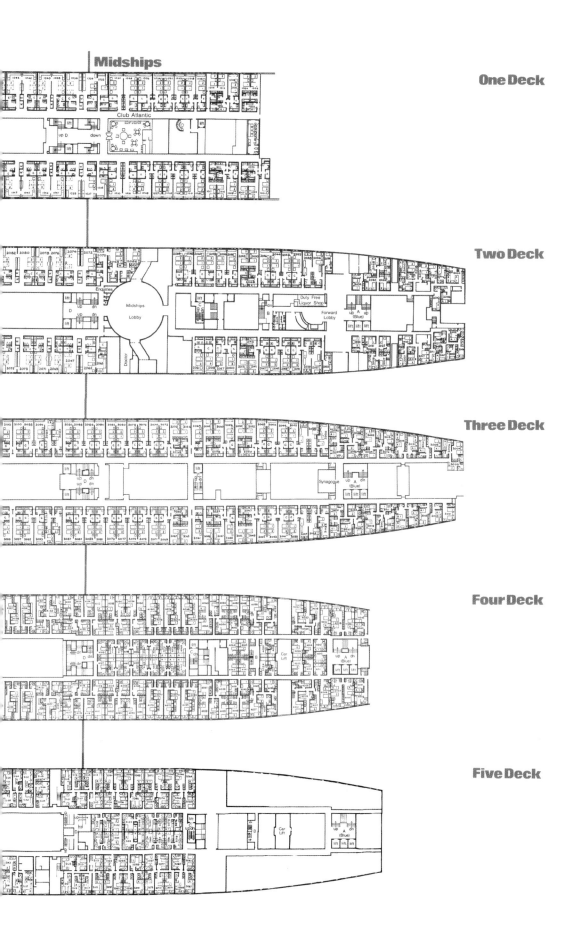

Midships

One Deck

Club Atlantic

up D   down

Two Deck

Enquiries

Midships
Lobby

Duty Free
Liquor Shop

Forward
Lobby

up A up
(Blue)

D
up dn

Doctor

Three Deck

up
up D dn

Synagogue

up A dn
(Blue)

Four Deck

dn

C

Car
Lift

up A dn
(Blue)

Five Deck

B   Car
Lift

up A dn
(Blue)

ABOVE A First Class
single cabin. *(Stephen
Payne Collection)*

rudder and shaftline bossings. Subsequent
tests were performed at the ship model tanks
of the National Physical Laboratory at Feltham,
Middlesex. Experiments in simulated North
Atlantic waves were an important part of
these investigations, and other tests included
some manoeuvring trials. As a result of these
studies and tests a modest bulbous bowed
hull form was finally adopted. In later years,
as the hydrodynamic effects of bulbous bows
became better understood, the bulb was
substantially enlarged. In both configurations
the bulb was designed to modify the flow of
water around the bow region in such a way
that it minimised the formation of a bow wave,
where the elevated water surface would have
caused significant additional drag. Advances in
marine engineering allowed the usual quadruple
shaftline arrangement to be compressed into
a more compact and economical twin-screw
configuration, which allowed *Queen Elizabeth 2*
to attain a speed of 32.46kt on her sea trials.

The ship was built under Lloyd's Register's
highest survey for classification +100 A1. She
also fully complied with all the relevant Board
of Trade, US Health Authorities and US Coast
Guard requirements for new passenger ships.
IMCO (Inter-Governmental Maritime Consultative
Organisation – now known as IMO, International
Maritime Organisation) fire safety regulations

particularly important for cruising. Several
large baggage areas were strategically placed
around the ship for the storage of large items of
baggage and 'not wanted on voyage' luggage.

Structural arrangements

The hull form of *Queen Elizabeth 2* was
developed and optimised through a
rigorous set of hydrodynamic tests. These were
undertaken initially at John Brown Shipyard's
own tank, where towed and subsequently self-
propelled model ship experiments were carried
out to configure appendages that included

BELOW *QE2* body
plan. *(Stephen Payne
Collection)*

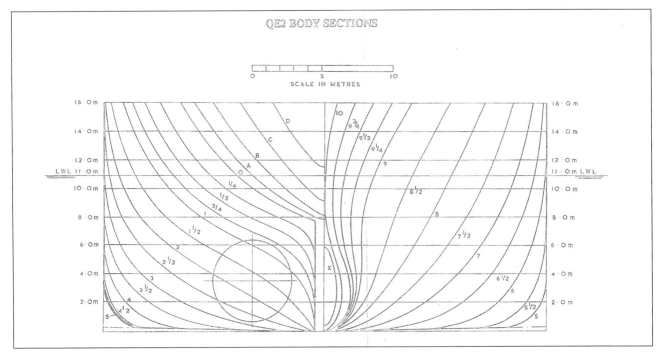

QE2 BODY SECTIONS

were also an important consideration for the design of the ship. Of all-welded construction, the hull was divided by 13 watertight transverse bulkheads into a level of compartmentation to comply with requirements as a two-compartment vessel. This allowed any two adjacent compartments to flood as a result of side-shell or other damage, and yet the ship would remain afloat under all normal loading and operating conditions. The ship was divided into 15 compartments which could be made completely watertight by closing 54 Hyston and 4 Hanston watertight doors, with control from the safety centre and the bridge.

Whereas steel was used for the hull up to main deck level, to minimise weight and restrict the draught and beam of the ship for port access and Panama Canal transits, the superstructure was fabricated from aluminium alloy, supplied by Alcan Industries Limited. Decks were framed longitudinally on the foyer deck and above and transversely on all other decks.

Another useful contribution to an increase in deck area resulted from a reduction of the 'tween-deck heights by about 6–9in per deck without detriment to the height of the decorative ceiling in the cabins, by careful pre-planning of the leads of piping and ventilation, together with redesigned structural girders which could accommodate the services without loss of headroom. This saving in height, together with a reduction in the height of the machinery spaces by similar pre-planning, finally resulted in a saving sufficient to provide an additional deck of accommodation.

In order to avoid alterations at a later stage, all general arrangements were drawn in large-scale detail even before the tender drawings were issued to the shipyards. Moreover, very early discussions were held with Lloyd's Register, the Board of Trade, the US Coast Guard, US Health Authorities, subcontractors and so on, so that their requirements and recommendations could be easily embodied within the design of the ship. The positions of all structural webs, bulkheads and pillars were also determined in the early design stage, and remained fixed as the surrounding details were developed.

This early work saved a considerable amount of time and allowed much of the piping, ventilation and so on to be prefabricated and

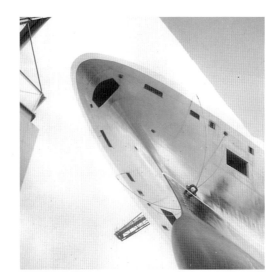

LEFT A fine study of the bulbous forefoot and stem, complete with its central anchor pocket. (Michael Gallagher Collection)

CENTRE A large Hanston watertight door under test. (Stephen Payne Collection)

BELOW Electro-hydraulic watertight door on the 'Burma Road' – a wide corridor that extends the length of the ship below decks for the crew to move machinery and equipment anywhere in the ship without having to go through the passenger spaces. (Tony Skilton)

erected on board the ship considerably earlier than would otherwise have been normal at the time. Except at the fore end of the ship, all decks were built completely level without normal camber or sheer. This greatly simplified construction and also helped to reduce building costs. By careful design of bulwarks and windows, and skilful use of colours, the level decks were not noticeable, and the flatness did not detrimentally affect the external appearance of the ship.

The deck beams were intercostal with continuous girders, and the steel structure was substantially strengthened forward within the double bottom to meet the heavy weather prevalent on the North Atlantic run. The bridge front was specially strengthened, as was the steelwork surrounding the tunnels of the two bow thruster units; these openings would otherwise have led to weakening because of the discontinuity of the structure. Additional material was also worked into the area surrounding the stabilisers and the region of the shaft brackets to offset the vibrations and higher stress conditions that occurred in this area.

The majority of the steel structure was fabricated from mild steel, but higher-strength 'E'-quality steel was employed around openings in the side shell, such as the ship's side doors, gangway doors, stabiliser openings and bow thruster openings. The utilisation of low-density aluminium for the superstructure reduced top weight by about half compared to steel, and enabled an additional deck to be incorporated into the design whilst maintaining the same dimensions for the ship as a whole.

However, a perennial problem concerning the steel/aluminium interface had to be surmounted. In the presence of moisture the join would form an electrolytic battery action, resulting in the rapid corrosion of adjoining metals. The modern practice, not available at the time of QE2's build, is to employ 'explosion-bonding' techniques, where the two metals transition on a intermolecular basis without any seam. In order to overcome this difficulty steel rivets were used for the joint, the two metals being separated by Camrex Camolite 999 insulation material. The thinness of the aluminium decks led them to be prone to buckling, which gave rise to a 'springing' effect when they were walked on. This was cured by the welding of a bead in a criss-cross pattern over the larger deck areas.

Lightweight girder system

During the 1950s Cunard investigated ideas that could potentially save weight in the design and outfitting of a future large passenger ship. To this end an intensive weight-saving exercise was conducted during the construction of the Line's Sylvania (1957; 21,989grt), which was built at the John Brown Shipyard. Lightweight furniture, plastic piping, glass reinforced plastic baths and showers, deck-covering materials and new construction methods for joinery work were all trialled, and the results compared in service to the traditional outfitting employed on the three earlier ships of the Saxonia series. Where successful, the new arrangements were incorporated into the design of Q4.

Concurrent with this work, investigations were undertaken with the British Ship Research Association (BSRA) to develop a new lightweight girder system. The resulting structural webs had large openings cut into them, and to compensate for the lost strength these webs were deepened somewhat. The overall effect was to produce a lighter structure with the useful addition of holes that could accommodate piping, ducting and cabling. This was also trialled on Sylvania and on Saxonia and Ivernia when they were reconstructed as cruise ships in 1962/63, emerging with the new names Carmania and Franconia, as previously noted. Girder and pillar positioning was determined very early on in the project, and it was decided to route cabling, ducting and pipe runs over alleyways and cabin bathrooms, where any loss of headroom would be generally acceptable. With these expedients, approximately 6ft was saved from the height of the superstructure, which led to a useful lowering of the centre of gravity and the ability to install an extra deck.

Despite these weight savings an additional 750 tons of weight was required low down in the ship to provide the requisite level of stability that was needed for the operational conditions, largely as a consequence of the machinery being so compact and light compared to previous ships. Rather than adding ballast, the extra weight was worked into the ship through increased scantlings, thickening up the side shell, double bottom and keel structure, and removing some of the openings in the floors. This resulted in an immensely robust structure that stood the test of time well and saved the ship from mortal harm on at least one occasion. Siting the main machinery slightly aft of midships was also beneficial for weight saving as it limited the amount of bending moment attributable to it, thus reducing the amount of structure that would otherwise have been needed to compensate for the bending moment. In fact the machinery position also suited the subdivision arrangements, so it really was an optimum solution all round.

Superstructure bonding

Whereas the old *Queens* were fitted with expansion joints within their superstructures, basically a cut in the structure to allow flexing, the openings created being sealed with a rubber gasket and sliding plates, the new *Queen* was designed to dispense with these troublesome structural discontinuities. Instead, the superstructure contributed to the longitudinal strength of the ship by being tied to it with riveting, the only area of the ship to utilise this form of bonding.

Outside decks

Passenger outside decks were traditionally wood sheathed, the underlying steel first being treated with Camrex non-oxidising preservative before the teak sheathing was bolted in position over welded stud bolts. Again to save top weight, thinner than usual teak sheathing was used, and because of the deck buckling previously referred to, this was pulled to the deck contour and locally filled with plastic fillers under the timber to minimise the amount of deck finishing required. As a preservative, All Weather Paints Ltd's Pitalac polyurethane sealer was applied to the decks beforehand.

Propeller and rudderstock

The ship's stern frame weighed 63 tons, whilst the propeller bossings weighed 116 tons and the rudder and rudderstock 90 tons. Castings for all these items were manufactured and supplied by Strommens Mek. Verk., Norway.

TOP The portside 'CUNARD' titles and strengthening doublers on the superstructure are prominent in this view of *QE2* at Southampton. *(Stephen Payne Collection)*

ABOVE Wood sheathing on outside decks. The forward end of Sports Deck beneath the starboard bridge-wing. *(Louis-Philippe Capelle Collection)*

BELOW *QE2*'s beautifully rounded stern seen whilst the ship lies at anchor at Moorea in the South Pacific. *(Louis-Philippe Capelle Collection)*

Queen Elizabeth 2 was the first ship in the world to have her rudder bearings lubricated automatically. An electrically controlled high-pressure system delivered 1 gallon of oil a day direct to the two main rudder bearings. The system was designed and installed by Higgs Lubrication of Glasgow, and was operated by an electrically driven pump capable of creating a pressure of 8,000lb/sq in. Every ten minutes, a measured quantity of 160SAE oil was delivered to each bearing.

Insulation and panelling

A ship of the size of *Queen Elizabeth 2* required large quantities of insulation materials to cover bulkheads and decks to form protective fire barriers. Cape Insulation Limited supplied their Rocksil and Composite materials for fire protection and thermal insulation purposes. Areas where these materials were used included the engine room, many of the public rooms and for the insulation of the ventilation trunking and ducts, whilst over 60 tons of Rocksil was additionally used in the insulation of refrigerated store rooms and cold chambers.

Extensive panelling, forming fire-resisting bulkheads, linings, ceilings and doors throughout the accommodation and public room areas, was supplied by Marinite Limited. Few if any of these Marinite panels were seen by the passengers or crew, being hidden under surface linings and finishes. On bulkheads, linings and doors the panels were faced with Formica laminated plastic, natural wood veneers or soft plastics. They afforded built-in protection in the form of non-combustible barriers, which in the event of fire were designed to confine the outbreak to the area in which it had started.

In many areas a lightweight decking insulation called Plasticell was employed. This consisted of a rigid expanded PVC material manufactured by BTR Industries which combined lightness with strength. This non-inflammable insulating material was specifically claimed to be non-absorbent and self-extinguishing in the event of fire.

Deck machinery

QE2's deck machinery included eight self-tensioning mooring winches, four on Two Deck forward and four on Two Deck aft. The winches were electrically driven via spur gears,

BELOW The promenade access passageway through the Chart Room on the Quarter Deck, midships starboard. *(Stephen Payne Collection)*

LEFT Mooring deck port aft on Two Deck. Mooring bollards, roller fairleads and warping winches are used for handling the ropes during mooring. *(Tony Skilton)*

FAR LEFT Capstan and controller. *(Tony Skilton)*

LEFT No 5 winch, aft end. *(Tony Skilton)*

arranged to take 400ft of 5in-circumference steel wire rope in five layers. Each winch was capable of 16 tons strain and 25 tons render. There were two electrically driven 25-ton warping capstans, one forward and one aft, duty from the barrel being 25 tons at 60ft/min and with slack rope at 180ft/min.

The cable lifters, two in number, were situated on One Deck forward, with the machinery room on Three Deck, the drive being supplied by vertical shafts. They were electrically driven, and the duty from each cable lifter was 60 tons at 60ft/min with a stalled load of 140 tons. One electrically driven anchor windlass was fitted on Three Deck aft, the duty from the cable lifter being 26 tons at 25ft/min. All of this deck machinery was supplied by Clarke Chapman & Co. Ltd.

Two 5-ton cranes were fitted on the Quarter Deck forward. The cranes were supplied by ASEA of Sweden and had an ASEA Thyristor control system. They could be operated by remote control and were fitted with an

automatic device for luff and slew motions, with hoisting speed at rated load being 210ft/min.

Two lengths, each of 120 fathoms and of 7in circumference, of Viking braidline nylon mooring rope were supplied by British Ropes Limited, as well as a quantity of 5in-circumference ML636 wire rope mooring lines, designed for use on the powered mooring winches, and a set of four Speed Seal couplings used during the connection of lines for the transfer of bulk liquids.

BELOW The forecastle with anchor capstans raised on individual platforms. *(Stephen Payne Collection)*

RIGHT Port bow
anchor in stowed
position and forward
mooring rope
arrangement.
(Tony Skilton)

Anchors

As built, *Queen Elizabeth 2* was provided with four anchors: three in the bow and one in the stern. The bow anchors weighed 12.5 tons each, whilst the stern anchor was 7.75 tons. The bow anchors were set in pockets port and starboard and one within the stem on the centreline. The latter was removed after a few years as it became frequently wedged in the stem by heavy weather; the pocket was sealed off, and the anchor was stowed on the forecastle. The stern anchor was also removed after a short period because of concerns that the cable would foul the anchor when deployed.

Safety systems

The safety control room situated at the centre of the vessel was manned by a trained operator at all times – in port as well as at sea. This 24-hour watch throughout the ship gave warning of any change from normal which might affect the safety of the ship and her passengers. Consoles with a complex array of instruments and alarms gave immediate warning to the watch-keeper before any significant emergency could arise.

SHOWCASING THE *QUEEN'S* ENGINEERING SUPPLIERS AND EQUIPMENT

Following *Queen Elizabeth 2*'s arrival in New York on 7 May 1969 after her maiden transatlantic crossing, Cunard took the opportunity to showcase the ship to the American media and local travel agents. The ship was concurrently used to showcase British engineering and the firms that had supplied equipment to her. Company representatives were flown out to the ship to act as ambassadors for their companies at various on-board receptions, whilst the British National Export Council and the British Marine Equipment Council published a booklet highlighting the companies and their equipment.

Watercraft

In 1954 Watercraft became the first company in the United Kingdom to have a glass-fibre lifeboat design approved by the regulatory authorities. The patented design process was successfully used to build many thousands of lifeboats that were used around the world. Today Watercraft is part of the Norwegian Norsafe group of companies, based in Aberdeen, Scotland.

Twenty Watercraft lifeboats were supplied to the *QE2*, comprising two special emergency lifeboats, four motor launches, eight lifeboats and six 'cruise launches' – tenders in modern parlance. All the boats were of glass-fibre construction, embodying Watercraft's system of two half hulls joined by substantial aluminium alloy bulb section backbone. All the boats were motorised, being powered by diesel engines.

The two 27ft emergency boats were coloured bright 'International Orange' for ease of recognition and were powered by twin Lister diesels, each driving a Dowty waterjet. This innovative system provided quick reaction times and excellent manoeuvrability. Watercraft's standard

ABOVE **Watercraft tender.** *(Stephen Payne Collection)*

RIGHT **Watercraft, with red emergency lifeboat. View from the port bridge-wing at sea.** *(Stephen Payne Collection)*

36ft hull was chosen as the basis for the motor launches and lifeboats. Whilst the lifeboats were not enclosed, the 140-person launches were provided with small cabins fore and aft and had awnings that could be rigged to bridge the gap. The six tenders were somewhat larger at 40ft length and had launch capacities of 60 people and 80 as a lifeboat. Each tender was powered by a single 6-cylinder 'V' form Parson-Cummings Vulture diesel, which developed 145bhp at 2,800rpm. The tenders were designed for excursion cruising and transfers, and had fore and aft cabin areas that were carpeted. Seating was aircraft style and linings were of Formica.

Since the *Queen Elizabeth 2* entered service in 1969 lifeboats and tenders have evolved into altogether different types of boats, with much greater capacity and different manoeuvrability characteristics.

RIGHT **Detail of the distinctive red emergency lifeboat on the portside.** *(Blair Skilton)*

ABOVE The Damage Control Centre Two Deck midships under construction. *(Michael Gallagher Collection)*

BELOW Firefighting systems control panel showing pressure gauges and valve indicators set within the firefighting pipe runs. *(Tony Skilton)*

Special emphasis was given to the fire integrity of the ship and precautionary fire measures. In view of the very satisfactory experience by British ship owners using the sprinkler system, this was again adopted, and the ship was built to the Method II system (some combustibles allowed but compensated by sprinklers) rather than Method I (no combustibles and no sprinklers). To reduce the fire risk, however, all bulkheads and ceilings were built from Marinite incombustible bulkhead material. The ship also virtually met the full requirements of the Method I system preferred by the Americans. This methodology is now obsolete, and an enhanced version of Method II is followed. During the building of the ship the IMCO requirements regarding fire precautions

were substantially amended and *QE2* was specifically built to comply with the requirements of the IMCO Fire Safety Committee of March 1967, although these were not mandatory for some years afterwards.

Whilst the main structure of the ship was entirely incombustible, internal areas were covered by an automatic fire sprinkler and alarm system, which in the event of a conflagration immediately activated the sprinkler system, giving a simultaneous visual and audible alarm in the safety control room, allowing the affected area to be pinpointed. In areas of the ship where it would have been unwise to have water sprinklers, detectors were fitted which could sense any minute changes in the atmosphere that indicated the presence of a fire, then raised the alarm. Such an incident would have been subsequently dealt with by the ship's firefighting party using special extinguishers.

The machinery spaces were extensively covered by foam spraying facilities, and the cargo holds and car decks were fitted with smoke and petrol vapour detectors, which activated and sounded an alarm in the safety control room and on the bridge, the location of the smoke or vapour being identified. Inert gas could then be released from the safety control room into the area concerned, thus smothering the fire. This equipment was used on more than one occasion during the ship's long career, saving her from catastrophic damage.

The water supply for firefighting was independent of the other water circuits on board, and there were two separate pumps for this purpose. Similarly, there were two dedicated pumps that fed the sprinkler system. The whole of the ship was divided into fire zones, with fire-resisting bulkheads and doors which could be closed by remote control from the safety room and the bridge to prevent fire from spreading. It was also possible to stop all accommodation ventilation fans throughout the ship from the safety room in order to limit the spread of fire through these conduits. An extensive emergency communications system covered the ship. Break-glass alarm pushes were situated in corridors and public rooms in such a way that it was always possible to see one of them.

The wheelhouse and bridge equipment

The layout of the original equipment in the wheelhouse and on the bridge-wings was based on an ergonomic arrangement that ensured ease and speed of operation for the watch-keepers.

In the wheelhouse, there were three main consoles: a pilotage console, a radar console

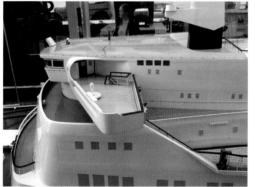

1 Ensign on gaff
2 Paying off pennant
3 Satellite aerial
4 Bosun's chair halliard
5 Electric sirens
6 Navigation lights
7 Radar
8 'Christmas tree' lights used when navigating in confined channels at night
9 Loud hailer
10 Air outlet

ABOVE Engine telegraphs.
(Louis-Philippe Capelle Collection)

(Stephen Payne Collection)

and a console for controlling various equipment located around the ship.

The pilotage console was located at the front of the wheelhouse on the centreline. It incorporated seven discrete functions: these were for the Stone Manganese Marine bow thrust controls; Tyfon whistle controls; Kwant engine room telegraphs; International Marine Radio VHF radio-telephone system; secondary steering controls and the gyro repeater; loudspeaking intercom systems to fore and aft docking positions; and a GEC-AEI Escort 654 radar, which was equipped with a 12in scanner and a 13in display.

Also centrally located was the radar console. This was based around a GEC-AEI Compact track computing radar that was cutting edge technology in 1969. This had a range of 48 miles and was equipped with a 12in scanner and a 16in display. It had a computerised interface that calculated the predicted tracks of a given number of targets and gave warning of any potential target entering a set closest point of approach circle. This was an early form of the modern-day ARPA (Automatic Radar Plotting Aid). There was also a Decca Navigator Mark 12 set and a very modern system that made use of the early polar orbiting satellites of the US Navy Navigation Satellite System (an early Global Positioning System) to give an accurate position fix to within 0.1 nautical miles. The equipment console which was described as the wheelhouse console was mounted on the aft bulkhead of the wheelhouse. It had the ability to control loudspeaking telephones at several locations in the ship; the bridge lighting switch panel; navigation light indicator; watertight door controls and indication; stopping of ventilation fans; stabiliser controls; and general alarms.

LEFT Propulsion controls. *(Tony Skilton)*

FAR LEFT AEI course plot on the bridge. *(Michael Gallagher Collection)*

LEFT Magnetic compass on the wheelhouse roof. *(Louis-Philippe Capelle Collection)*

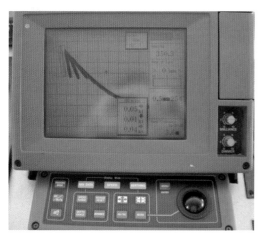

FAR LEFT Speed measuring Doppler Log. *(Tony Skilton)*

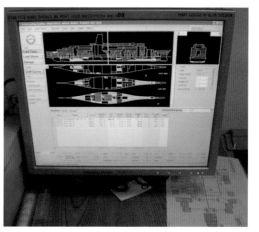

LEFT The ship's Stability Computer was calculated twice daily. *(Tony Skilton)*

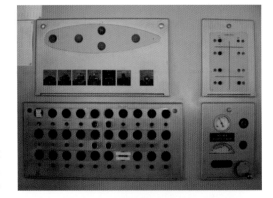

RIGHT Navigation lights control panel. *(Tony Skilton)*

BELOW Watertight doors control panel. *(Tony Skilton)*

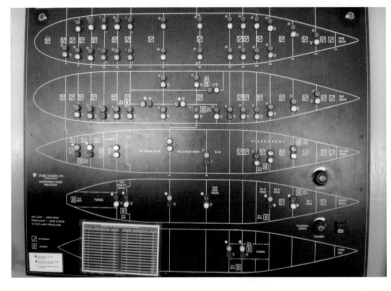

Primary steering of the ship was carried out from a steering pedestal stand situated on the centreline between the pilotage and radar consoles. In the chart room behind the wheelhouse there was an additional console which encompassed the following equipment: crystal chronometer; Kelvin Hughes echo sounder; Marconi echo sounder; master clock for the ship's clock system; gyro course recorder; Sal Junger log; International Marine Radio/ITT Loran A and C long-range position indicator; and a Marconi Lodestar II automatic direction finder.

In addition, mounted in the chart room, were the Marconi Forecaster Receiver complete with facsimile printer type 649/L/DA and a computer output printer, which recorded telegraph orders and output information from the computer weather routing program. On each bridge wing were two consoles contained within protective enclosures with hinged tops. The first console provided intercommunication between the bridge wing and the wheelhouse, bridge wing and a lifeboat control system, and VHF radio-telephones. The second provided engine room telegraph information including propeller rpm, rudder angle indication, whistle activation and bow thruster control.

RIGHT The helm. *(Tony Skilton)*

FAR RIGHT The Chart Room. *(Tony Skilton)*

FAR RIGHT Bridge wing manoeuvring console in the diesel era. *(Blair Skilton)*

THE DECCA NAVIGATOR COMPANY LTD

When the new *Queen Elizabeth 2* was outfitted with a Decca Navigator Mark 12 receiver, which the company claimed was the most accurate marine navigation aid in the world. In 1949 *Queen Mary* was the first Cunard liner to be equipped with a Decca Navigator, closely followed by the remainder of Cunard's passenger fleet. The system provided coastal navigational fixing information in north-west Europe, North America, South Africa, India, the Persian Gulf and Japan.

The Navigator produced a red, green and blue set of coordinates which when transferred to a suitably referenced chart could be used to provide a triangulated fix – the three coordinate system being more accurate than just two.

Decca Navigator has long been superseded by the now common satellite Global Positioning System (GPS). The system was based on hyperbolic radio signals being transmitted from beacons between 70 and 129kHz. The system provided greater accuracy than the competing LORAN system but could not match GPS. Range was variable, but up to 400 miles from the transmitting beacons was possible.

Racal Electronics acquired Decca Navigator in 1979 as part of a deal for Decca Radar. By the end of the 1980s it was not economic to continue the Navigator service, so Racal approached the UK Government, and thereafter it was funded by the General Lighthouses Authority (GLA) with Racal managing it, until final phase-out between 2000 and 2001.

ABOVE Decca Navigator. *(Stephen Payne Collection)*

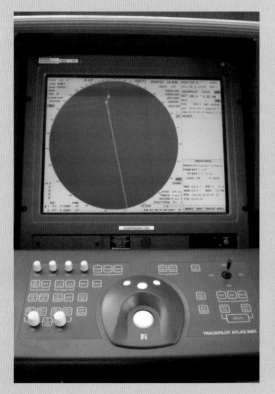

LEFT AND BELOW The Decca Navigator was eventually replaced with a modern SAM radar display. *(Tony Skilton)*

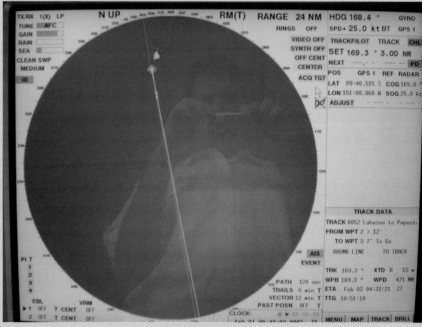

POSITIONS INDICATED ON TV
MONITORS ARE NOT SUFFICIENTLY
ACCURATE FOR OPERATIONAL
PURPOSES

Chapter Four

Power behind the throne

Advances in marine engineering and naval architecture allowed the 65,000grt Q4 design to provide more space for more passengers than the 83,000grt *Queen Elizabeth* (1940). State of the art in every sense, *QE2*'s machinery and technical outfit was designed to give the ship a cutting edge and an acceptable return on the investment to build her.

OPPOSITE Chief Engineer Paul Yeoman at the engine room telegraphs of the diesel-electric ship. *(Tony Skilton)*

It was envisaged that the ill-fated 75,000grt Q3 liner would have been propelled by four screws driven by 200,000shp geared steam turbines with steam supplied by eight boilers arranged in two boiler rooms at 850psi and 950°F. Estimated fuel consumption was 800 tons per day compared with 1,050 tons on *Queen Elizabeth*, whilst 146 engine room crew would be required against 220 on the *Elizabeth*. The whole premise of the subsequent 65,000grt Q4 design was that the latest ship would be dual purpose and would be able to operate on two screws, with a much more compact and economical 120,000shp power plant. The original plans foresaw four boilers and five turbo-generators, but this was revised to three boilers and three turbo-generators in December 1964 in order to reduce costs to allow the shipbuilding contract to proceed. Power was also slightly reduced to 110,000shp when it was ascertained that the optimised hull would only require between 85,000 and 95,000shp for the desired 28.5kt service speed, the excess 15,000shp being a useful margin in times of extreme inclement weather. At service speed fuel consumption would be 520 tons per day and the compact machinery plant would only require 93 engineering staff.

Turbines

Queen Elizabeth 2's pair of 55,000shp turbine sets were of Parmetrada design, manufactured by the shipyard John Brown &

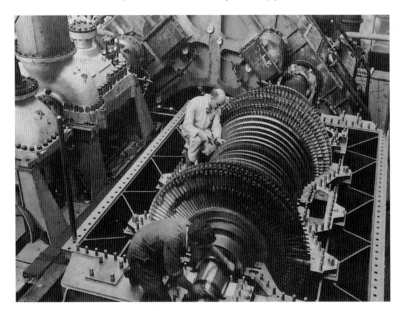

Co. Ltd. Double reduction helical gearing was employed. The high-pressure turbines used one Curtis wheel (rotating blades followed by a fixed nozzle) followed by eleven single row impulse stages and rotated at a maximum of 5,207rpm, whilst the low-pressure set based on double flow impulse/reaction elements rotated at 3,192rpm. At 100% steam flow not less than 80% of ahead torque at 50% revolutions was available from the stern turbines. Separate nozzle units were welded directly into the main inlet casing and connected with pipes to the nozzle control chests. This enabled detailed control to be maintained at different stages within the turbine, allowing optimal conditions and maximum efficiency to be provided. Steam passed through the turbines from aft to forward when steaming ahead and opposite when running astern.

The turbine casings were cast as a double shell with the nozzle units carried in clusters in inner shells supported from the outboard casing. The rotors were cast as a single solid chromium-molybdenum-vanadium forging which was subsequently machined. Within the high-pressure turbine the nozzles and blades were cast either from molybdenum-vanadium-niobium stainless iron, molybdenum-vanadium stainless iron or molybdenum stainless iron depending on location and associated ambient temperature, the more exotic alloys being deployed where conditions were the harshest. The low-pressure turbine section was fed with steam via a crossover pipe and incorporated six stages of impulse blading and four reaction stages. The high efficiency stainless steel impulse blading was specially designed by Parmetrada, as was the reaction blading. The latter was of cutting edge technology with molybdenum stainless iron blading, the final stages being carefully twisted and tapered on the vortex principle, shielded on the inlet edge to negate water erosion.

The astern turbines comprised two turbines on each propeller shaft connected in series, one connected to the high-pressure pinion and another on the corresponding low-pressure pinion. A single high-pressure astern Curtis wheel was installed in the high-pressure turbine, whilst two rows of astern blades were provided in the low-pressure section.

FISHER GOVERNOR DIVISION

The Fisher Governor Division of Elliott-Automation Control Valves Ltd manufactured a full range of control valves and control equipment for use in industrial applications, such as petrochemical and power generation, under licence from Fisher Governor Company of Marshalltown, Iowa, USA. The firm supplied over 150 automatic fluid control valves to *Queen Elizabeth 2* for the control of the ship's engine room services and the distribution of steam and water throughout the ship. The valves ranged in size from 1in to 16in bore and were manufactured at the company's premises in Rochester (Kent) and Cowdenbeath (Scotland).

All the main engine services were controlled with the valves fitted on the turbine steam ranges, control and lubricating systems, regulating temperature and pressure by flow adjustment. The valves were also an integral part of the emergency turbine shut-down system.

The closed feed system was automatically controlled through piston-operated valves fitted in the steam lines leading to the feed pumps, ensuring that a constant differential pressure was maintained by regulating the speed of the feed pumps across other Fisher valves, which controlled boiler feed water flow into the boilers.

The level of water in the deaerator was kept constant by two butterfly valves which controlled the flow into the system, or alternatively diverted water from the deaerator should the need arise. The evaporators, which produced fresh water from sea water, had Fisher valves controlling the steam supply into the brine heaters and the sea water supply into the evaporators.

Steam supply for the ship's hotel services, such as the laundry and air-conditioning systems, was extensive, and Fisher reducing valves controlled the steam pressure to these services. Further valves and pressure controllers were used in the fresh water distribution main and in the supply of compressed air for engine room cleaning and for the driving of machine tools. To ensure the correct pressure regulation of hot and cold fresh water and sanitary water, Fisher valves and 'Wizard' pressure controllers were installed at each deck level.

The majority of the valves were of the diaphragm or piston-actuated type, mostly with single port bodies with material of manufacture dependent on usage. Gunmetal was used for the sea water valves whereas stainless steel and stellite (a high cobalt, self-hardening steel) were extensively used elsewhere, including for four valves in the turbine drain, the laundry steam supply valves and the air-conditioning supply valves.

Elliott-Automation originated as a firm of instrument makers called Elliott Brothers, which was founded in 1800, Elliott-Automation itself being formed as a private company in 1950. In 1967 Elliott-Automation was acquired by English Electric Co., becoming part of GEC in 1968 as GEC-Elliott-Automation. The subsequent story of GEC would require a book in itself, and is beyond the scope of this potted history.

BELOW Fisher Governor Systems. *(Stephen Payne Collection)*

Boilers

Each of the three Foster-Wheeler ESD boilers built under licence by John Brown Engineering (Clydebank) Limited had a dedicated bled-steam air heater and a waste heat economiser to maximise efficiency and reduce energy losses. Automatic temperature control of the internal boiler dampers allowed the combustion gases to be directed over the super-heater tubes in a predetermined optimum manner across the complete range of firing operation, the degree of utilisation being dependent on load requirements. Three electrically driven fans, each with a rating of 400kW, one for each boiler, supplied combustion air at the maximum rate of 81,000cu ft/min. This air was drawn from the fan house on the top deck where the funnel rested, the air passing in the opposite direction to the boiler exhaust gases in the boiler casing. Seven side burners were fitted to each boiler, spraying hot heavy fuel oil into the combustion chamber, and the furnaces were fully water-

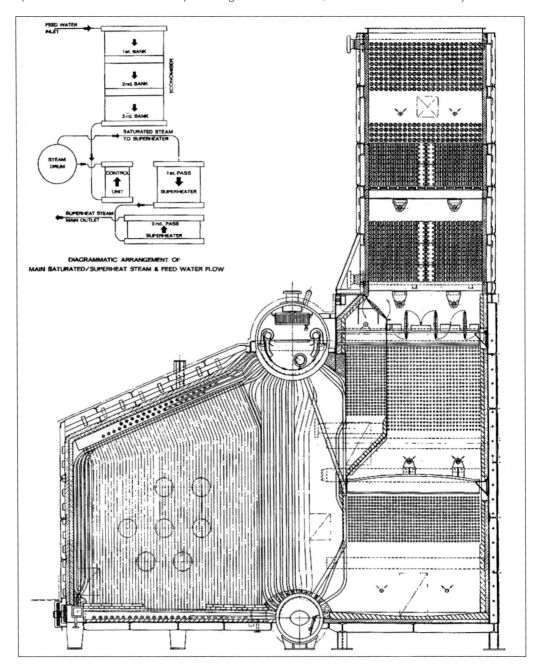

RIGHT Foster-Wheeler boiler. *(Cunard)*

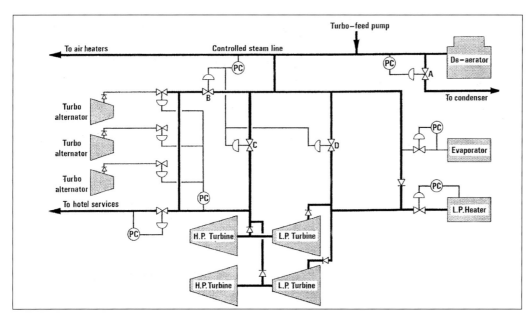

LEFT **Steam valve control system.** *(Stephen Payne Collection)*

cooled with close pitched tubes. Each complete boiler was double skinned, with the space between the inner and outer casing acting as a conduit for the pressurised combustion air to pre-heat it prior to entering the furnace chamber. The boilers had an impressive turn-down ratio of 14:1, which meant that they could produce fourteen times the amount of steam when operating at maximum output compared with the minimum output, and any value in between. This provided great flexibility with economy when compared to earlier less sophisticated plants, and at normal operating conditions the fuel consumption was 0.82 tons/mile compared to 1.66 tons/mile for *Queen Elizabeth*. The boilers were designed to operate at 1,000°F but were limited to 950°F in operation, and each one had a normal steam output of 231,000lb/hr, which could be increased to 310,000lb/hr when conditions warranted. The super-heaters were of convection type and were located remotely from the furnaces, being protected by several banks of steam-generating tubes. The complete boiler, super-heater and economiser tubes were arranged with a wide inline separation to ensure ease of maintenance and cleaning. Soot blowing was effected by a comprehensive system manufactured by Clyde Bergemann. Each of the three boilers weighed 278 tons, at the time the largest marine boilers in service.

The boilers were located within a single compartment, with the three turbo-generators in the adjacent forward compartment and the propulsion turbines in the corresponding aft compartment.

Gearboxes

Queen Elizabeth 2's main propulsion gearboxes were described as double reduction (i.e. two stages), dual tandem, fully articulated with all rotating elements of helical pattern. Marine gearboxes are notoriously fickle and require exacting design and manufacturing tolerances. For this reason the French Line engineered the superlative *Normandie* (1935), arch rival to Cunard's *Queen Mary* (1936), with turbo-electric drive, negating the need for gearboxes by using electrical means to effect the required reduction in speed between the turbines and the propellers. *QE2*'s gearboxes were state of the art, exceptionally engineered components built to the highest tolerances. The pinion diameter ratio was specially chosen to ensure pinion deflections were substantially less than usually employed in the merchant maritime sector. The dynamically balanced primary and secondary pinions of the two stages were machined from nickel-chromium-molybdenum alloy steel forgings and they were within tolerance for Lloyd's Register's requirements for surface and root stresses from gear tooth loadings. The turbines were connected to the pinions using double-ended fine-toothed flexible couplings to minimise out of alignment

RIGHT Propellers and rudder. (Stephen Payne Collection)

FAR RIGHT Stone Manganese six-bladed propeller. (Bruce Peter Collection)

BELOW Prop shaft tunnel. (Tony Skilton)

vibrations. Axial movement of the couplings were limited by substantial spring clips, which permitted the teeth to be easily inspected when necessary by disengaging the clips and sliding the sleeve axially. Secondary quill shafts were connected to its pinion by a single-ended, fine-toothed coupling.

Propellers

The twin shaftline arrangement was unique for an express liner and at 55,000shp per shaft was the highest rated mercantile marine installation. The earlier *Queens* had four-bladed, fixed-pitch propellers nominally rated at 40,000shp each, but *QE2* employed six-bladed propellers rotating at 174rpm to absorb the higher power and limit vibrations. The propellers had a projected area of 23.5m^2 and were manufactured by Stone Manganese Marine Ltd; they were cast from Superston 70 nickel-aluminium bronze and had a diameter of 5.79m and a pitch of 6.6m, whilst weighing just over 32 tonnes each. When the ship was delivered the two propellers cost over £500,000. Four propellers were supplied; two as working units on the ship and two to be kept ashore as spares. The propellers were attached to 250ft-long propeller shafts, which were in turn connected to the output shafts from the propulsion gearboxes.

SPEED/FUEL CONSUMPTION DATA

Speed: maximum 32.5kt sea trials as a diesel-electric ship; service 25–28.5kt

Fuel consumption: 18.05 tonnes/hr, or 433 tonnes/day.

- The ship's fuel oil tank capacity of 4,381 tonnes was sufficient for 10 days' sailing at 32.5kt, equalling 7,800 miles.
- As a diesel-electric ship, each gallon of fuel moved the ship 49.5ft compared with the previous steam turbine plant, where each gallon of fuel moved the ship just 36ft.
- As a diesel-electric vessel, the ship could decelerate from a speed of 32.5kt full ahead to a stop in 3min 39sec, whilst covering a distance of 0.75 nautical miles (1.39km).
- As a diesel-electric vessel, the ship could accelerate from standstill to full speed astern in 12 minutes, reaching 19kt astern.

Electrical generation

Three AEI turbo alternators were installed that each produced 5,500kW at 3,300 volts at 60Hz. At the time of the ship's commissioning they were the largest turbo-alternators built for maritime deployment, and it was the first time that such a high voltage was used in a marine application. Two 350kW emergency alternators were also provided by AEI but driven by Paxman diesel engines. The 3,300-volt network directly fed high-power motor consumers but was reduced to 415 volts and 240 volts for lower-power applications throughout the ship. The alternators were designed for automatic operation, running up

ALKALINE BATTERIES LTD: EMERGENCY SUPPLY BACK-UP BATTERIES

Alkaline Batteries Ltd of Redditch was a leading British nickel-cadmium alkaline battery manufacturer formed in 1947 – and ultimately owned by Chloride. Using the tradename Alcad the company supplied a number of batteries to *QE2*, including one weighing 8 tons. This battery was used as the primary black-out back-up and was capable of supplying 600 amps at 240 volts for 30 minutes to power emergency lighting, essential navigation systems and watertight door indicators. Alcad control equipment was used to maintain the charge on this huge battery. The secondary back-up was two emergency diesel generating sets driven by Davy Paxman engines, which in themselves were started using two 24-volt Alcad batteries formed from 20 DL-27 high-performance cells; all fitted with control and associated charging equipment.

Other Alcad battery applications included the supply of batteries for starting the four diesel lifeboat launches and two rescue boat engines; switch-closing of circuit breakers using a 184-cell battery; emergency radio station power from three 20-cell batteries; and low-voltage electrical services including

public address using two 41-cell batteries. In all, 21 Alcad nickel-cadmium batteries were installed on board.

After a number of changes in ownership the company is now part of the French Saft Group (Saft-Nife), based in Sweden, manufacturing in the UK having ceased in 1993. Products are still branded with the Alcad name.

LEFT **Alkaline batteries.** *(Stephen Payne Collection)*

to speed and then joining the network through the switchboard unaided following command from the central machinery control room. The high-power 3,300-volt applications included twelve motors rated between 290 and 1,000hp such as the 1,000hp bow thruster motors, the 525hp forced draught fans for the boilers and the 700hp refrigerating compressors.

Fluorescent lighting was extensively used on board the ship, including for cabin lighting. This had the double benefit of reducing the direct energy required and also reducing the air-conditioning load, owing to the lower heating effect of the lighting when compared to the incandescent filament type. A comprehensive telephone system with 1,200 lines was installed with a semi-automatic switchboard, which included a special speaking clock feature. The complexity of the system was unparalleled at the time of the ship's entry into service, and installation was made easier by constructing it in modular form at the point of manufacture and then fitting the completed harnesses directly into the ship. Cabins were provided with British and American electrical sockets for personal low-power equipment at 240/110 volts, a six-channel music system and air-conditioning control.

Computer control

Much was made of *Queen Elizabeth 2*'s innovative computer installation developed by Ferranti. At the time of her delivery in 1969, the ship had the most sophisticated computer system ever to be used in a merchant ship. It was the first to combine technical, operational and commercial functions at sea. The installation, based on an Argus 400 computer supplied by Ferranti Ltd, was a progressive development – the outcome of over two years' investigation and research in which Cunard Line cooperated with the British Ship Research Association, the National Research Development Corporation, Ferranti Ltd and the shipbuilders.

Initially the computer system had six main functions: data logging, alarm scanning, machinery control, weather routing, the prediction of fresh water requirements and stock control. Later, as the operational profile of the ship became defined and the computer became more 'experienced', with its databanks contributing to its knowledge, the computer's functions were extended to other data-processing needs of the ship in

BELOW The engine control room in the steam era. *(Bruce Peter Collection)*

its role as a floating hotel, such as the billing of passengers' personal bar accounts. The machine was also employed for stock control of hotel consumables. Apart from set functions, the Ferranti programming was designed to allow the machine to assist with intermittent bespoke tasks through additional routines. The computer was installed in a special room next to the main control room, and the ship's engineer officers and technicians were specially trained to operate the system.

Computers were also used for planning functions whilst the ship was being commissioned. The final run of a PERT program, which had been used on a monthly basis since April 1968 by Cunard to monitor and control the critical latter stages of the ship's commissioning, took place on a 1900 Series computer in the London computer centre of International Computing Services Limited. It was the first time that a computer's network analysis techniques had been adopted to cover the commissioning and working up period of a ship. A 1900 PERT computer was also used by the builders for planning and construction coordination.

Control system engineering

Marine control systems were rapidly evolving at the time *QE2*'s contract was placed in December 1964. Computers and electronic switching were just beginning to find applications in industry and offered the possibilities of allowing centralised control and monitoring of complex machinery, with the dual advantages of reduced manpower requirement and more precise operation. Cunard's most recent ship before *QE2* had been the *Sylvania*, last of the *Saxonia* quartet built for the Canadian run and delivered in 1957. The machinery installation of the ship was conventional, following established practice, and it certainly couldn't give a lead for the new superliner. It was therefore decided to appoint specialist consultants Automatic Control Engineering to assist with the coordination of instrumentation and control systems. Following an evaluation period, during which various available systems were analysed, it

was decided to adopt AEI's Marecon control equipment and protocols. Equipment suppliers were required to provide their equipment with a suitable interface that allowed connection to the Marecon system. Automatic control was grouped and effected from three main control rooms: turbine control room, main control room and damage control room. Each was provided with various consoles and an Engineer's Desk with intercommunication equipment to local control stations and the principal control rooms, including the bridge. A computer printer was located on each desk providing access to all the relevant information for that station.

The glass-fronted turbine control room was dedicated to the operation of the propulsion system, and principally controlled and monitored the turbines. At the control consoles essential data from the boiler room was available so that the turbines could be prudently operated. Each of the two shafts was controlled from two manoeuvring levers, which managed the steam flow through the turbines. The first lever controlled the first ahead steam nozzle and the aft turbine, whilst the second lever sequentially engaged the second through to fourth ahead steam valves. Activated by the control levers, pneumatic pressure transmitters directed signals to the valves according to pre-set conditions in normal operation, with emergency override functionality when rapid control was required. Various safety interlocks were incorporated and turbine drains and recirculating valves were automatically controlled. Turbine lubrication and bleed steam arrangements were other important functions that could be performed from the consoles.

ABOVE Cylinder lubricator. *(Tony Skilton)*

The main control room regulated the operation of the three huge boilers. Combustion control was effected primarily by feedback from the main steam line pressure.

Machinery lubrication

Fourteen grades of lubricants were originally employed on board the ship from delivery, all supplied by Castrol Industrial, Marine Division. The lubricants ranged from highly refined oil for the main turbines (35,800 gallons of Perfecto Heavy) incorporating inhibitors to more standard types for dressing wire ropes. Rustilo 630 corrosion preventive compound was used to coat the internal surfaces of important components, such as the main gearboxes, pipelines and so on.

Refrigeration plant

Refrigerated stores were kept in 23 separate chambers, each one maintained at a different temperature. Refrigeration was provided by four six-cylinder reciprocating compressors operating, with Freon 22, at 1,750 rev/min and driven by 65hp motors. This equipment was supplied by the Carrier Engineering Co. Ltd. A direct expansion system was employed, each chamber being fitted with a unit-type air cooler through which the air in the room was circulated using constant speed fans. Each chamber was thermostatically controlled to its pre-set temperature, and an automatic system of defrosting was featured.

Passenger and crew accommodation was air-conditioned throughout by a Carrier single-duct, high-velocity system employing terminal reheat, which enabled a complete range of cabin temperatures to be selected. A volume of 500,000cu ft/min of conditioned air was distributed through the cabins and public rooms by means of a continuous slot opening, which was designed to blend in with the surrounding decor and minimise noise and draughts. For the air-conditioning and ventilation system, 20 Vokes Autorolls automatic air filters were supplied.

Fresh water production

Adequate fresh water production was crucial to the ship's successful operation, and three Weir flash evaporators produced 1,200 tons of fresh water every 24 hours. This enabled *Queen Elizabeth 2* to be self-sufficient in fresh water for both boiler feed and domestic hotel services. As required by health authorities, the domestic water was chlorinated to kill off any bacteria.

Rudder and steering gear

Queen Elizabeth 2 was fitted with a single semi-balanced streamline rudder weighing 70 tons, positioned at the end of the centreline skeg. The rudder was constructed in Norway by A/S Strommens Vaerksted. The steering gear employed to turn the rudder was a traditional hydraulic four-cylinder ram type supplied by Brown Brothers and powered by two pumps driven by Kapak metric cage induction motors rated at 175hp at 1,175rpm. The rudder was normally operated by all four rams with one pump, the second pump being held in reserve in case of a failure. Seamless transfer between pumps was a feature of the installation. The pumps were of the variable delivery type with a rated pressure of 4,500psi and were controlled by a modern servo mechanism, which greatly simplified the design of the steering gear and dispensed with the heavy levers and springs associated with earlier set-ups. The electric control system did away with the need for

BELOW Fresh water system evaporators.
(Tony Skilton)

mechanical amplification, and led to much smoother operation of the steering gear and rudder movement.

The rudder bearings were lubricated by an automatic lubricating system rather than a drip feed arrangement – *QE2* was the first ship in the world to have automatic rudder bearing lubrication. The system was supplied by Higgs Lubrication, and was an electrically controlled high-pressure delivery system that dispensed oil in 75-second bursts every ten minutes directly to the main rudder bearings, 1 gallon of oil being used every 24 hours. Four high-pressure pumps were employed by the system to overcome the bearing pressure and the hydrostatic back pressure due to the rudder immersion.

Stabilisers

Four Brown Brothers stabilisers were fitted to *QE2* to counteract the ship's rolling motion. The fins each had an area of 70sq ft and were housed in enclosures called fin boxes set transversely across the hull, two each side of the ship, being of the modern swing-back type (rather than with fixed transverse deployment).

These were controlled by a gyro system supplied by Muirheads.

When the fins were deployed, they were pushed out of their boxes by hydraulic rams, and a Brown Brothers control system activated further hydraulic rams that constantly changed each fin's attitude to provide either upwards or downwards force (hydrodynamic lift) to counteract the rolling motion of the

BROWN BROTHERS & CO. LTD: ANTI-ROLL STABILISERS AND STEERING GEAR

Brown Brothers & Company was founded in 1871 by Andrew Betts-Brown, a Scottish engineer from Edinburgh, in partnership with his brother. Andrew Betts-Brown devised and perfected the concept of hydraulic steering gear and telemotor used to effect rudder movement for the steering of ships. For many years this type of equipment was one of the company's best sellers, and the equipment supplied to *QE2* utilised many modern innovations, such as electric motors, over the original design but was otherwise classic in its form. Another of the firm's famous products was the Denny-Brown ship stabiliser, developed by Sir William Wallace in association with Sir Maurice Denny of Wm Denny Brothers of Dumbarton. This constituted hydrodynamic fins contained within an enclosure called the fin box that could be extended beyond the ship's hull using hydraulic actuators. The fins' angle of attack to the incoming flow around the ship could be altered by further hydraulic actuators, thus producing upwards or downwards hydrodynamic lift that could be used to oppose the rolling motion of the ship. The control system altering the angle of attack of the fins to provide the requisite counterforce was crucial to the success of the equipment. Gyroscopes were originally used, but these mechanical systems have over time been replaced by solid state technology, which is predictive rather than reactive.

The first passenger ships to receive fin stabilisers were the Cunard combination passenger-cargo ships *Media* (1947) and *Parthia* (1948). These small, all First Class ships were notable rollers on the North Atlantic. They were retro fitted with a pair of stabilisers in 1953, and the results were so spectacular that Cunard decided to equip *Queen Mary* and *Queen Elizabeth* each with two pairs of fins in 1958 and 1955 respectively.

A stabiliser collaboration agreement between the Denny-Brown companies and the German firms of AEG and Deutsche-Werft was signed in 1960, whereby each company would contribute its particular expertise in the design of future stabilisers. *Queen Elizabeth 2* was equipped with two pairs of fins set in fin boxes that were arranged transversely across the ship. *QE2*'s four stabilisers measured 6ft by 12ft and were controlled by a gyroscope. This used the effect of precession to generate an electrical impulse that controlled the hydraulic pumps that actuated the fins. A roll reduction of 60% was achieved, albeit with a slight increase in ship drag.

The *QE2*'s electro-hydraulic steering gear was a ram-based arrangement with four hydraulic cylinders actuating a cross tiller, in two opposing sets arranged in an 'H' configuration. Two pumping units were installed. Under normal circumstances only one was required to operate the four rams, although both units could be employed and configured as required in exceptional conditions, such as when extreme weather was encountered. Each unit was powered by a 175hp electric motor running at 1,175rpm driving a Vickers VSG SP.30 pad pump. Each servo-controlled pump could deliver 4,500psi, and the design and control was such that it negated the normal heavy springs previously associated with steering gears.

The installation provided ample redundancy for the control of the 75-ton single rudder, which was manufactured in Norway by A/S Strommens, Vaerksted. It was notable that *QE2* was the first ship that had her rudder bearings automatically lubricated. This was achieved using a high-pressure system employing three supply lines, designed by Higgs Lubrication of Glasgow, which delivered a gallon of oil every day to the bearings in 75-second bursts every ten minutes.

ship. Rolling of 22 degrees without fins could be brought down to around 3 degrees with the fins deployed. The stabilisers could be deployed in any combination, the number of fins used at any one time being dependent on the severity of the conditions. The number of deployed fins is usually kept to a minimum, as each fin introduces a degree of increased drag which raises fuel consumption, but against this the enhanced hydrodynamic performance attributable to a stabilised ship has to be compared with that of the rolling equivalent. It should be noted that rolling is only one of the possible six ship motions and that stabilisers can only effectively control this one. Pitching (pivoting radial up and down motion of the bow and stern) is much in evidence in Atlantic swells, but is barely influenced by stabiliser action. In common with many passenger ships, passive bilge keels (sometimes called rolling chocks) were fitted to each side of the ship in the region of the turn of the bilge to offer some resistance to rolling. These are long wedge-shaped protrusions that are orientated to the streamline flow-lines of the water as it passes around the hull to minimise drag effects.

Bow thrusters

Queen Elizabeth 2 was provided with two Stone Manganese Marine bow thrusters driven by AEI electric motors rated at 1,000hp, operating at 263 rev/min. The thruster propellers had two controllable pitch blades and were 6.55ft in diameter, each producing a lateral thrust of 11 tons. The two thruster tunnels were separated by about 4ft and were fitted at each end with 'butterfly'-type swing doors, hinged longitudinally across the diameter. The tunnels were flush mounted at both ends without scallops or grids and the butterfly action doors were hydraulically operated. In the open position for side thrust operation, half of the doors resided within the tunnel, whilst the other half projected outside the hull. The doors allowed the forward end of the underwater hull to present a flush and smooth entry, and thus maintain the streamline flow in order to minimise drag. The bow thrusters were used to assist with berthing and unberthing operations, but in reality were rather underpowered for

ABOVE One of the four Brown Brothers stabilisers. *(Stephen Payne Collection)*

the purpose. Operation of the doors and the thruster motors was directly controlled from the bridge. With only a single rudder and with fixed-pitch slow-reacting twin propellers at the stern – and no stern thrusters – manoeuvring invariably still required tug boat assistance. Modern cruise ships are fitted with thrusters and podded arrangements that largely dispense with the need for tugs.

LEFT Stone Manganese bow thruster. *(Stephen Payne Collection)*

Chapter Five

Renaissance: the big refits of 1986–87 and 1994

Within two years of entering service, *QE2* was radically altered by the first of many refits. The ship was never the same for long, always being modified and improved. But two refits stand out as game changers. The first was re-engining in 1986–87, to sort out her reliability issues once and for all. The second took place in 1994, the Project Lifestyle refit. This would make the ship more successful than she had ever been previously.

OPPOSITE The nine diesel exhausts are manoeuvred into position. *(All photos Michael Gallagher Collection unless credited otherwise)*

Re-engining and refurbishment in 1986–87

After an extensive six-month rebuilding at Lloyd Werft Bremerhaven in 1986–87, the Cunard flagship *Queen Elizabeth 2* sailed into Southampton proudly flying the Queen's Award for Industry, having achieved 35kt en route through the English Channel, bringing with her unfounded Blue Riband speculation and numerous problems.

Since her introduction into service the *QE2* had undergone considerable modification, with several structural additions and countless decorative changes. Operationally she followed an annual pattern of an extended winter voyage, usually in the form of a World Cruise, and strenuous five-day transatlantic crossings interspersed with a few short European cruises and a number of extended transatlantic voyages to the Caribbean. However, by the mid-1980s the stigma of recurring mechanical unreliability plagued her operation, including instances of complete power failure and numerous electrical blackouts, which at times seriously undermined her economic viability. With a daily fuel consumption of around 500 tons at a service speed of 28.5kt, the original steam propulsion plant began to appear increasingly archaic, uneconomic and, ultimately, the Achilles heel of an otherwise successful operation. Cunard, being mindful of the *Queen*'s prestigious image

and replacement cost, rejected the new-build replacement option and instead initiated a series of comprehensive re-engining studies, which lasted some two and a half years.

Phase 1 of the detailed evaluations began with Cunard inviting engine manufacturers and shipyards worldwide to make individual re-engining proposals, following a meeting held at Southampton in July 1983. Only a brief outline of the performance criteria required was given to the 11 initial competitors, so that as wide a range of alternative solutions as possible would be forthcoming. These conditions were:

(i) The proposed propulsion plant was to be capable of meeting the operating profile of the ship (including a 15% margin) using no more than 85% of the maximum continuous rating of the installed plant.

(ii) Noise and vibration levels of the converted ship were not to exceed those of the existing steam propulsion plant in order to ensure a high degree of passenger comfort.

(iii) A fully automated, unmanned engine room design was required in order to ensure maximum reliability and enhanced maintainability.

(iv) The maximum out of service time for conversion was set at seven months.

Individual competing groups of shipyards or shipyard/engine builders could incorporate

BELOW A queen once more.

and take full advantage of their respective technologies, ideas and methods. An important aspect was that as a condition of participation each engine manufacturer was required to accept responsibility for the design and performance of the entire propulsion plant. In parallel, Cunard themselves considered a broad range of alternatives in order that the submitted proposals could be adequately evaluated. These included maintaining the existing steam plant for the remainder of the vessel's projected life, installing a combined steam and diesel plant, a combined steam and gas turbine configuration, diesel mechanical using diesels and a gearbox driven shaftline, diesel-electric, thus dispensing with the gearbox, and even the possibility of conversion to coal and coal slurry burning to raise steam for continued steam turbine operation. The operational profile of the vessel that was given to the competing groups aptly demonstrated the demanding nature of the ship's operation:

Speed range (in kt)	Operating time (% time)
0–10	7
10–15	1
15–20	5
20–22	4
22–24	16
24–26	18
26–28	49
	100

Maintaining the existing plant as a baseline (maintenance, labour, insurance and other ship expenditures), which was assigned the incremental cost ratio of 1, the three most feasible options as identified by Cunard could be compared. All provided a life expectancy of an additional 20 years, with the conversion downtime of between three and seven months. These were:

(i) Retention of the original propelling machinery with upgraded boiler performance by incorporation of combustion automatic control and performance monitoring. Replacement of two steam turbo-alternators with diesel alternators to reduce steam consumption. Cost ratio 1.89. The inherent problem of requiring all three boilers to be in steam with limited maintenance possibilities would still have been present.

ABOVE **Steamship**
QE2 **alongside Ocean**
Terminal in Ocean
Dock, Southampton.

(ii) Same as (i) but with the installation of three diesel alternators, replacing two turbo-alternators to provide additional flexibility. Cost ratio 2:02. Inherent boiler problems as with (i).

(iii) Re-engining, utilising diesels for both propulsion power needs and the generation of electrical auxiliary load. Incorporation of waste heat and new fuel treatment plant. New propellers. Cost ratio 3.42.

Of these three alternatives, option (iii) provided by far the most significant projected reduction in operating costs, coupled with significant increases in redundancy and reliability. It was concluded that the economic argument to re-engine was therefore valid, and the feasibility studies progressed to the second phase. The reasons for re-engining were quite clear: increased voyage profit; increased life cycle cash flow; increased reliability; maintenance of a prestigious image; notwithstanding a cost-effective alternative to new construction.

Phase II was therefore embarked upon. This called for further in-depth technical appraisals of the various re-engining proposals. Having decided to go diesel, the various different conceptual diesel arrangements available were carefully compared. Basically the choice was between geared diesels with constant- and variable-pitch shafts and an integrated 'Power Plant' based on a diesel-electric configuration. Technical analyses of speed and power requirements, hotel steam loads, electrical

demands and vibration conditions were undertaken by specialist firms and Cunard, with the data being fed back to the engine builders. Exhaustive evaluation of over 15 different submitted proposals by 7 manufacturers led to the final conclusion that a diesel-electric plant would best fulfil all the necessary conditions and criteria demanded. The final phase of the feasibility study involved evaluating the proposals from the three engine builders and associated yards left in the running. Ultimately the decision was taken by the Cunard Board to proceed with the project, and the conversion order was placed with Lloyd Werft at a contract price of US$115 million to be undertaken over the winter months of 1986/87, with the project lasting 179 days.

LEFT The gutted former boiler and engine rooms are ready to become the two diesel engine rooms with nine engines.

RE-ENGINING PROJECT TIMETABLE

27 October 1986	*Queen Elizabeth 2* arrival at Bremerhaven.
28–31 October	Cutting of access openings for shipment of parts in and out of the hull.
29–30 October	Removal of old funnel.
31 October–7 November	Removal of original six-bladed fixed-pitch propellers and tailshafts with the ship dry-docked in Lloyd Werft's Kaiserdock II dock.
4–13 November	Rudder repair work, with the original rudder being retained.
25 November–4 December	Installation of new five-bladed controllable-pitch propellers and energy recovery 'Grim Wheels'.
4–8 December	Installation of both main 45MW propulsion motors.
18 December 1986–21 January 1987	Installation of nine medium-speed diesel engines within two engine spaces created by gutting the original boiler room and engine room.
19–22 January	Installation of the main 10kV switchboard.
13–20 February	Installation of the supporting structures for the exhaust gas boilers and silencers.
27 February–3 April	Test running of new engine plant alongside at the outfitting quay.
11–18 March	Reconstruction of funnel, enlarging the structure to accommodate the larger exhausts and utilising as much of the former structure as possible.
3–7 April	Final dry-dock work.
7 April	Inclining experiments to determine the vessel's stability and stability margins following the conversion works.
8–15 April	Sea trials in the North Sea to fully test the new propulsion plant and auxiliary systems.
15–26 April	Completion of all outstanding work.
25 April	Redelivery to Cunard Line.

The electric link

The adoption of the diesel-electric drive for re-engining provided a number of distinct advantages over the other options studied, such as greatest reliability owing to the possibility of redundancy and 'power station'-type operation, less noise and vibration by resilient mounting of diesels, and greatest flexibility owing to optimisation of load conditions. Finally, installation work was simplified by the flexible siting of machinery arrangements, lack of reduction gear alignment, lack of clutches and the facilitation of resilient mounting. These factors significantly outweighed the disadvantages of initial greater capital cost and slightly higher operating costs as compared with the straight diesel option without the electrical plant.

Diesel-electric drive was not a new concept. The Hamburg-America Line's *Patria* of 1938 (16,600grt) was the first large diesel-electric passenger ship. Electric drive, albeit with steam, was used for the French Line's transatlantic liner *Normandie* of 1935 (80,000grt) and P&O Line's *Canberra* of 1961 (45,000grt). However, the technology associated with the electrical plant had advanced enormously since those installations, especially with the advent of micro-electronics, and thus the earlier systems bore little resemblance to *Queen Elizabeth 2*'s outfit.

The *Canberra*'s system was regarded for much of her long life as the classical AC propulsion system. It consisted of a frequency-variable voltage arrangement, with the voltage and frequency being varied in unison so that a constant voltage/frequency ratio could be maintained, that is constant volts/cycle, whereby the magnetic flux in the propulsion motors was constant throughout the operating range. This permitted direct speed control from the turbines by simply varying the speed, since the AC motors ran at a speed determined by the frequency of the turbine generator-supplied voltage.

Modern systems permit direct control within the electric link, hence allowing the diesel generator sets to be run at constant speed. This is very advantageous for diesel prime movers as they can be run at their optimum speed. Control is effected through a variable frequency converter of which there are two types, cyclo and synchro. Cyclo converters can generate a variable frequency supply from a fixed frequency supply, which may be used to power either synchronous or asynchronous motors with the ability to produce a relatively smooth motor torque throughout the speed range. However, a deteriorating output voltage waveform is produced with increasing frequency, and this limits the usable output frequency between a third and half of the input frequency. Synchro converters consist of two conventional, fully controlled thyristor bridges, connected via a decoupling link choke. The bridges form two separate converters, supply and machine. The former is connected to a constant voltage and frequency AC system such as that supplied by a constant speed diesel generating set. The supply converter produces a controllable DC link current, which the machine converter controls to produce a rotary 'magnetomotive' force in the stator of the propulsion motor. Thyristors within this machine converter are switched in sequence to provide the magnetomotive force in the correct orientation as the stator field advances upon stator rotation. Synchro converters played an integral part in the *Queen Elizabeth 2*'s new propulsion system.

The new propulsion plant

The *Queen Elizabeth 2*'s new propulsion plant consisted of nine diesel generator sets driving two synchronous electric motors. The prime movers were nine-cylinder MAN

BELOW *QE2* **re-engining machinery plant.** *(Stephen Payne Collection)*

LEFT *QE2* **midship section in way of engine room.** *(Stephen Payne Collection)*

B&W L 58/64 four-stroke, medium-speed, large-bore diesel engines, with a heavy fuel oil consumption of 123g/hph producing a cylinder output of 9 × 12 15kW. Four diesel units were arranged athwartships in a forward machinery space with five similarly arranged in a compartment immediately aft, both spaces being directly below the ship's funnel. The engines used fuel grade IF 380 (Bunker 'C') and was heated under pressure to 140°C for injection, being akin to road tar at room temperature. The myriad of exhausts were led up through the original casing without the disturbance of passenger areas. A considerably larger funnel was required to house the uptakes compared to the boiler exhausts, but it was generally of the same form as the original funnel and retained the forward iconic forward-facing wind scoop feature. All of the engines were resiliently mounted to the ship structure using layered rubber elements angled at 45° with the aid of supports bolted to the engine base and

BELOW LEFT One of the new diesels is manoeuvred within the machinery space cavity.

BELOW Cathedral of power – one of the new engine rooms.

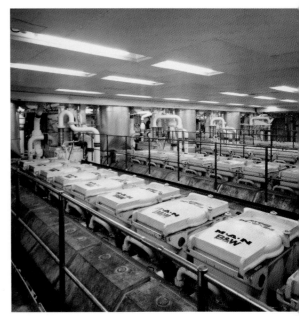

foundation. In the low-frequency range the dynamic forces produced by the engines were no longer transmitted to the structure, as they were absorbed by the mountings and balanced by the inertial forces produced by the entire engine bodies themselves. Mounting the engines in this way after exhaustive testing at MAN's Augsburg factory ensured that noise and vibration levels were minimised and kept within the stipulated levels. It is reported that on start-up the engines jumped around quite violently until they became balanced as their speed increased. In fact, during tests on one engine the turbocharger broke loose; this fault was corrected by additional stiffening. For safety, specialist Hoerbiger crankcase relief

ABOVE LEFT The new funnel under construction within one of Lloyd Werft's sheds. Notice part of the wind scoop to the right.

ABOVE The new funnel is positioned over the nine diesel exhausts.

LEFT The magnificent diesel-era funnel. (Louis-Philippe Capelle Collection)

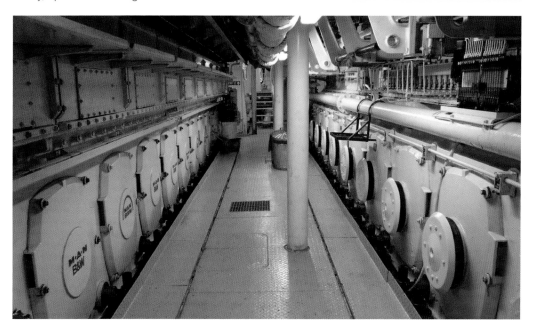

LEFT Aft engine room engines, each weighing 220 tonnes. (Tony Skilton)

ABOVE Engine and propulsion systems controls, with five engines on load.
(Tony Skilton)

BELOW Central cooling system controls and alarms. *(Tony Skilton)*

valves were fitted to all nine engines. At service speed, *QE2* carried enough fuel for 12 days' continuous sailing, but at the slower, more economical speed of 20kts, she could sail for 30 days, or two-thirds of a circumnavigation of the world.

Each engine was directly connected via a Vulkan-Rato flexible coupling to a GEC 10.5MW alternator, being driven at 400rpm. This method was used in preference to resiliently mounting the alternator sets on a common skid with their attendant diesel engine. Each engine and alternator set combination weighed 220 tonnes. The alternators fed a 10kV main switchboard, which was the highest tension marine application to that date, all supplied by Field and Grant, part of a £3/4 million contract placed by GEC as part of their own supply. The switchboard consisted of synchronising controls, metering and instrumentation, incorporating nine vacuum circuit breakers

RIGHT One of the scrapped steam turbines removed during re-engining.

fed from the generators. The outgoing section supplied the main propulsion motors and 3kV transformers for domestic hotel with loads of between 5 and 10MW through similar vacuum circuit breakers.

The two main 44MW 144rpm propulsion motors each weighed 350 tons, and were the largest ever manufactured by GEC Machine. They provided a useful increase of 10,000shp in

ABOVE One of the two 350-tonne electric propulsion motors is hoisted on board.

ABOVE The stripped-out engine casing during re-engining. *(Late Edward Divett Collection)*

BELOW One of the propulsion motors is lowered down the funnel casing.

BELOW The middle section of one of the motors. *(Tony Skilton)*

ABOVE Alfa-Laval heavy fuel oil separators.
(Tony Skilton)

BELOW The old doormat trick to keep the shafts pristine and prevent rust – port propeller shaft running at 140rpm.
(Tony Skilton)

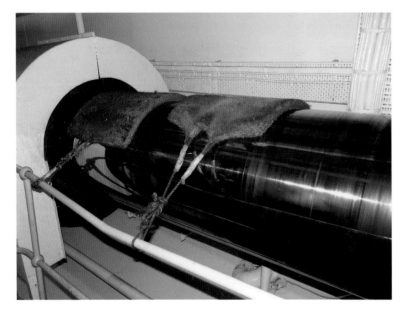

back-flushing Duplex filters with a heavy fuel oil flow rate of 17m³/hr, which achieved a filtration degree of 34 microns. These filters ensured that harmful particles could not reach the sensitive injection equipment.

Nine Alia-Laval WHPX 410 lub-oil separators were installed, and Bull filters similarly ensured the purity of each independent lubrication system, with type 6.33/SK filters giving a 34 micron filtration and a flow rate of 248m³/hr. An Alfa-Laval centralised Engard computer-controlled cooling system, with 15 titanium plate heat exchangers, was employed to economise on pumping energy by analysis of the operating conditions and the optimum selection of pumps. Fuel oil capacity was reduced from 6,425 tons to 4,640 tons. Two 11MW synchro converters were supplied for starting the propulsion motors and providing slow-speed operation of the vessel. This enabled combination-type operation up to a speed of 18kt solely by varying shaft speed. The new controllable-pitch propellers in fact required only two shaft speeds (constant revs) to provide full variable speed: 72rpm below 18kt and 144 above. Redundancy built into the plant enabled a service speed of 28.5kt and full hotel electrical demands to be met with only six of the nine generator sets in operation, therefore allowing for a continuous rotating maintenance programme to be adopted. The complete combination formed a 95.5MW integrated power station, supplying power for all the vessel's electrical needs.

The last links in the propulsion chain were the propellers. The original fixed-pitch screws were replaced by two Lips five-bladed, high-skew controllable-pitch propellers. At 5.8m these were of the same diameter as the originals, but were nearly 10 tons heavier at 42 tons each. They were in fact the most powerful CP propellers to be put into service at that time. At the service speed of 28.5kt, consumption was 380 tons per day: this equated to 50ft/gallon.

One of the areas identified as causing vibration with the original machinery was the propellers. The low hull impulse characteristics of high-skew propellers significantly reduced this on the converted ship. Two new shaft lines connected the screws to the propulsion motors. These two propeller shafts were 80m long, of solid forged steel, and were 590mm in diameter.

propulsion power for maintaining speed in heavy weather. These motors were lowered into the ship through the old engine casing aperture, slid aft on temporary rails and positioned on the new thrust blocks. The motors were so huge that even with the propellers set at zero pitch, 7.3MW was absorbed purely to turn the shafts. They were designed in a segmented configuration so that they could be broken down into a number of sections, facilitating maintenance and repair work. Seven Alfa-Laval FOPX 613 separators were supplied to maximise the performance of the diesel engines with high-density heavy fuel oil. Each engine was supplied with fuel through Boll & Kirch type 6.50 fully automatic self-cleaning,

LEFT *QE2*'s famous short-lived Grim Wheels. *(Stephen Payne Collection)*

Riding on the ends of these shafts behind the propellers, there were two Grim Wheel energy recovery vanes. These seven-bladed vanes had a diameter of 6.7m (15.5% greater than the propellers themselves), weighed 14.5 tonnes and were designed to rotate at about 15% of the propeller speed, that is 22rpm.

Being lightly loaded, the vanes posed no hull impulse vibration problems. The Grim Wheels were supplied as a package by Lips with the propellers, and calculations predicted a 4% energy contribution or a 10-ton daily fuel saving. In combination with the new screws, a total energy reduction of 7–8% at 28.5kts was anticipated. Unfortunately, whilst returning to Southampton from Bremerhaven at the conclusion of the refit, travelling at 35kt, the Grim Wheels broke up, leaving only two vanes attached to each wheel. Being completely unbalanced in this condition, severe vibration resulted, and Cunard had no option but to remove the remaining blades upon arrival at Southampton so that the vessel could proceed with her maiden voyage as a motor ship. Divers were sent down to sever the blades and the ship sailed with only the central boss intact. Without the Grim Wheels the propellers were no longer of optimum design, so within a few months new propeller blades were cast. These were fitted during an emergency dry-docking – and the Grim Wheel experiment was not repeated.

The re-engined *QE2* could now accelerate from 0 to 16kts in five minutes and 18.07kts was achieved at eight minutes. At full speed the ship had the ability to stop within a mile and three minutes compared with 5 miles and considerably longer beforehand.

The fuel consumption figures for different speeds as measured in 2002 were:

Speed (kts)	Fuel consumption (tonnes/day)
18	160
18.5	164
19	169
19.5	174
20	180
20.6	186
21	193
21.5	200
22	208
22.5	217
23	228
23.5	239
24	251
24.5	264
25	279
25.5	295
26	310
26.5	327
27	345
27.5	366
28	387
28.5	412
29	440

Waste heat recovery and boiler installation

New waste heat recovery arrangements on board produced a thermal efficiency of 88%, whilst the total system efficiency of the whole plant was designed to be a commendable 75%. Recovery of waste heat was centred around cylinder cooling water, charge air heating and exhaust gas. Eleven new boilers were installed on board *Queen Elizabeth 2*, supplied by Sunrod. Nine of these boilers were directly associated with the diesel engines, being exhaust gas fired, and were arranged within the original engine casing; they had a maximum steam output of 4 tons per hour. This was used for a number of services, including fuel heating, air-conditioning, hotel heating and fresh water generation. Two Sunrod auxiliary donkey oil-fired boilers were provided to augment the exhaust gas boilers when the vessel was in port or when slow running with fewer than four diesels in operation. These boilers had an output of 25 tons per hour at 7 bar. Steam in excess of requirements was dumped into condensers. Fresh water generation was accomplished by utilisation of waste heat steam into four Serck vacuum flask evaporators with a combined output of 1,000 tonnes per day. A reverse osmosis system was also employed with a capacity of 450 tonnes per day. Fresh water tankage was decreased from 4,201 to 2,534 tonnes and water ballast from 3,724 tonnes to 4,617 tonnes.

Automation and control

The engine control room was the nerve centre for the ship and was continuously manned for the control of the engines, generators, propulsion motors, synchro converters, transformers, switchgear, steering gear, propeller pitch and pumps. An extensive engine room control console provided monitoring for over 2,500 points through a GEC GEM 80 Uni-Control microprocessor. A mimic diagram of the complete system (generation, distribution and propulsion) was installed, and this alerted the engineers to the performance of the whole network through Uni-Control displays and alarms. A second small console on the navigating bridge provided direct bridge control of the propellers. Woodwood electronic controls were chosen to manage the operation of the diesel electric plant. A 501 Power Manager monitored the power required and power available to maintain peak fuel efficiency. The 501 Automatic start/stop sequencer received commands from the power manager during normal operation whilst a 501 Remote back-up start/stop sequencer provided essential

BELOW The engine control room of the diesel-electric era ship. *(Tony Skilton)*

manual operation for back-up. Nine Woodwood 43027 modular analogue controls provided speed control and soft loading/unloading along with electrical and mechanical synchronisation. These could be automatically controlled by either the main 501 unit or the back-up. An Avel KD uninterruptible 8 kVA supply system played a vital role in maintaining AC power supplies to the monitoring equipment in the event of failure of the alternator supply, ensuring that system control was never blacked out in the event of engines tripping off-line.

Refurbishment of passenger areas

After the signing of the re-engining contract, Cunard commissioned extensive refurbishment to be undertaken concurrently with the technical refit, thus increasing the value of the contract to $163 million. Of this figure, roughly 25% was attributable to such refurbishing works, and in consequence very few parts of the ship were left untouched. Many of the public rooms were modified to varying degrees. The Tables of the World Restaurant serving Tourist class gave way to a new £2 million restaurant called the Mauretania. Seating was provided for 1,000 diners. It was envisaged that on all but the most heavily booked voyages a single sitting system for dining, as operated by the three first-class restaurants, would prevail. However, with the drive to maximise revenue and sell every cabin, if not every berth, the restaurant reverted to its two sitting Main and Late configuration. Old prints from the days of the first *Mauretania* (1907–35), a detailed model and an oil painting of the same were used for decoration, creating a pleasant dining atmosphere. In a new move, a dance floor was provided in this and the first-class Columbia Restaurant. Both the Queens and Princess Grills were also redecorated.

By far the largest change on board was the total rebuilding of the famous Double Room. As built, this was a vast lounge on two levels. The lower level extended the width of the ship and access to the narrower upper level within the first tier of superstructure was via a grand curved staircase positioned at the aft end of a large open well that connected the two levels.

ABOVE Re-engining nearing completion during 1987.

LEFT The 'G' Stairway looking towards the Grand Lounge following the 1987 refit. *(Stephen Payne Collection)*

BELOW The Grand Lounge after the 1987 refit.

LEFT The initial incarnation of the Yacht Club in place of the old Double Down Bar prior to 1994.

CENTRE The Yacht Club and Bar post-1994. *(Stephen Payne Collection)*

The upper level of the lounge disappeared in 1972 when the shops were relocated there. During the 1987 refit the existing lower lounge was transformed into the new Grand Lounge, and this provided terraced seating for the viewing of stage entertainments. An extending stage replaced the original fixed stage, but two new curved staircases clumsily extended horseshoe fashion down its sides. Originally predominantly red, the room was now dark blue. Following the refit, the upper level shopping arcade sporting expensive-name boutiques extended further aft into a new aluminium deckhouse (Boat Deck aft), the roof of which was clad in teak forming a new recreation deck. The old Double Down Bar was completely rebuilt and renamed the Yacht Club, the space being enlarged by incorporating an adjacent promenade, made possible by the deletion of the original aft curved bulkhead. The overwhelmingly popular computer centre, which was previously located on Boat Deck, was relocated to Two Deck in order to provide more space and facilities. An Adult Centre, Teen Centre, enlarged Sports Centre with electronic golf, Board Room and remodelled One Deck pool with jacuzzis were further changes incorporated to enhance the vessel's facilities. Eight new veranda Penthouse suites (bringing the total to 36) were built on the last remaining area of crew deck forward of the funnel housing. These accommodations were at the top end of the range, and their occupants dined in the specially extended Queens Grill. Passenger capacity had increased by 16 to 1,870. A team of 150 workers systematically worked through the 1,100 cabins, refurbishing and renovating as required. All cabins now featured direct-dial satellite telephone lines and bilingual verbal clocks. First Class cabins now

LEFT The One Deck Pool aft. *(Stephen Payne Collection)*

had Grundig televisions that were fitted with video machines, whilst stereos and safes were also installed in each room. Twenty-one miles of new carpeting was laid during the refit. In total, £4 million was spent on upgrading the accommodation and facilities for 1,050 crew members, consolidating and re-equipping the galleys and hospital, and installing new Dreher laundry equipment, which handled some 30,000 items per voyage.

The refit entailed the removal of 4,500 tonnes of scrap material and 6,700 tons of new equipment and materials were added, most of this entering the ship through the engine casing with the aid of specially chartered Smit Tak floating cranes. At times 1,200 workmen were engaged on the ship.

Return to service

The Queen Elizabeth 2 returned to Southampton on 28 April 1987 after an eventful voyage from Bremerhaven, at times running at 35kts. Having attained this sort of speed it was only natural that questions of the Blue Riband would be asked, and it was very surprising to learn that Cunard announced that they were in fact considering an attempt. (How things had changed from the Cunard attitude of the 1930s, when such an idea would not have even been suggested, Cunard having rejected the Blue Riband trophy when the Queen Mary captured the record from Normandie). However, QE2 never did attempt the record.

Although accepted by Cunard, the ship was hardly ready for service. Employees acting as guinea pigs for the return trip were treated to mostly cold food, whilst the majority of the public rooms and cabins remained in considerable disorder. Several hundred workmen continued to work as members of the press and invited guests toured the vessel. On 29 April, before sailing on her second maiden voyage to New York, the ship played host to 500 underprivileged children and HRH Princess Diana.

Reports from the QE2's maiden voyage as a motorship were perhaps unjustified. Maiden voyages of most large passenger ships are difficult. Passenger numbers had sensibly been limited to 1,200, but there was some

ABOVE A funnel and an old propeller amongst the piles of scrap.

BELOW Resplendent in her new look.

ABOVE *QE2* post re-engining before the Magrodome was removed in 1994.

BELOW **The Double Room as configured after 'Project Lifestyle'.**
(Stephen Payne Collection)

difficulty in finding suitable cabins. Showers, lavatories and telephones were not working in many areas, and passengers were advised not to drink the water. Even the master, Captain Lawrence Portet, lost his cabin when the Cunard Commodore Ridley commandeered it! A hundred shipyard workers and 150 Cunard-contracted staff continued to work throughout the trip. By Friday, three days out of Southampton, one of the four swimming pools was operational, but the jacuzzis were still out of action and the air-conditioning continued to drip on diners in the Queens Grill. At one stage, the ship made an alarming 15° list to port, but this was corrected as soon as the Commodore complained. Service began to improve and there were fewer cold dishes. However, some passengers said that the vessel definitely appeared noisier than before. Some 200 passengers booked on the third voyage had their trip cancelled as their cabins were not ready, having been occupied by Lloyd Werft workmen. But the ship soon settled down in service, and as a very much more economical, viable and reliable passenger ship. After a few months, with the impending withdrawal of the diminutive *Stefan Batory*, the *QE2* became the only passenger liner on the Atlantic, a true ocean greyhound and definitely 'the only way to cross' until the advent of *Queen Mary 2*.

'Project Lifestyle' refit, 1994

In 1994 Cunard sent the *Queen Elizabeth 2* back to Germany, this time to Blohm & Voss in Hamburg, for a significant rebuild of the hotel side of the ship. This was codenamed 'Project Lifestyle', and was masterminded by MET Studio of London in association with John McNeece Ltd. MET recruited a large specialist team to work alongside its own staff for nine months on the full masterplan of the ship, which involved the redesign of most of the public spaces, and a rationalisation of how the Cunard brand was presented. The MET team began the project by thoroughly researching the history of Cunard, comparing contemporary cruise liners from competing lines with the *QE2* and the *QE2*'s changing

passenger demographics to clearly understand the company's strategic objectives.

MET determined that although existing passengers loved the ship, they found her original two-class design conception was too limited, and the ship needed to be 'opened up'. MET attempted to redefine the vertical and horizontal circulation routes in order to allow a return to the tradition of 'promenading' the whole length of the ship, as well as giving good daytime to evening passenger movement flow, allowing for maximum on-board revenue generation at all times of the day. MET also felt that overall the public areas needed a major upgrade, so that everyone who sailed in her could retain a sense of occasion.

The new interior designs for the ship included integrated commissioned artworks, providing a narrative which referred to Cunard's history alongside many specially commissioned and exclusive materials and finishes. All aspects worked together to form a sophisticated colour palette, giving the ship the unified and timeless elegance it demanded.

Whereas Cunard Line's original intention with *QE2* in 1969 had been to shun the past and look forward to the future, eschewing any on-board references to the previous *Queens*, MET now advocated a 'Heritage Trail' with an avalanche of memorabilia and nostalgia. Nothing exemplified this more than the placing of a huge model of Cunard Line's venerable RMS *Mauretania* (1907) at the apex of the split corridor on Quarter Deck at the head of 'D' Staircase opposite the Caronia Restaurant, where three tapestries depicting the launch had once hung.

During the 21-day US$45 million refit in the

ABOVE The Midships Lobby after 'Project Lifestyle'. *(Stephen Payne Collection)*

BELOW Post-'Lifestyle' refit of 1994, *QE2* departs Sydney during a World Cruise.

was added along the superstructure somewhat above the dark blue/white demarcation boundary, and a rampant Cunard lion, in gold outline, was emblazoned on the forward superstructure above the 'CUNARD' sign. For a short time the Trafalgar House emblem of three house flags was also applied to the superstructure sides above the aft end of the stripe. Two new 45ft catamaran tenders, one on each side of the ship, were installed on the Boat Deck, these being considered useful for fast transfers ashore. In the event, the new catamarans and the exterior rebranding in royal blue, including speed stripe and lions, were all soon removed, but the new interiors fared much better, being largely retained unchanged for the rest of the ship's career.

Later refits

In late 1999, during the first refit under Carnival's stewardship (13 November to 9 December), the opportunity was taken to repaint *QE2*'s hull in the original charcoal-grey colour, reversing MET Studio's 'Project Lifestyle' rebranding. This was part of a move towards consistent branding across the Cunard fleet, and *QE2*'s fleet-mate *Vistafjord* was similarly rebranded, losing her grey hull and being given

dry dock in Hamburg, MET had a team of 12 designers and project managers on site, with two of the team remaining on the ship for part of the subsequent World Cruise to oversee the teething problems and snagging that occurred. MET was jubilant that in the first year of sailing after redefinition, on-board revenue increased by 33%; no mean feat.

The refit included recarpeting some stairs with dark royal blues, whilst the hull lost its charcoal-grey (black) hull for a second time, to be repainted in Royal Yacht *Britannia* dark blue. A three-tone gold–red–blue 'speed stripe'

the venerable Cunard name *Caronia*. Public rooms and cabins were renovated where necessary and three new suites were added, the former Radio Room on Boat Deck portside and the Doctor's Suite and Hotel Manager's Suite on Two Deck starboard side off the Midships Lobby becoming the Caledonia, Carinthia and Aquitania passenger suites.

The *Queen Elizabeth 2*'s last major refit was undertaken at the Lloyd Werft Shipyard at Bremerhaven between 2 and 20 May 2004. During this period normal surveys and renewals were undertaken, including some steelwork repairs within various tanks and elsewhere on board. With the ship in dry dock, the underwater hull was cleaned of marine growth and fouling before being repainted with new brick-red anti-fouling paint. The hull and superstructure were also repainted and the extensive teak-sheathed passenger open decks were repaired where necessary, especially those areas where the caulking between planks had deteriorated, allowing water to seep between the wood and the deck itself. Technical upgrades and general maintenance included changing the ten controllable-pitch propeller blades, repairs to the auxiliary boilers, and an overhaul of the two bow thrust units and the lifeboats and tenders.

A significant safety upgrade took the form of the installation of a water mist firefighting system in the engine room. Traditionally, Halon was used in machinery spaces, but its deployment had to be carefully considered as anybody caught within the spaces where it was discharged without breathing apparatus would inevitably be killed. During a refit in 2001 the Halon system was replaced with carbon dioxide as halogens were phased out because of concerns relating to their effect on the Earth's ozone layer. Carbon dioxide was not a panacea as it too could endanger life after discharge, and so the change to water mist was effected as soon as practicable. The modern water mist system acts in a different way to carbon dioxide/Halon, working by quickly cooling areas to the point where combustion is no longer sustainable rather than starving the fire of oxygen. Water mist can be quickly discharged as it does not endanger personnel. On the hotel side a new passenger service area was incorporated into One Deck, and many passenger public room areas were refurbished and repaired with much new carpeting being laid where required. Public toilets also received attention and some passenger cabin bathrooms were upgraded.

BELOW *QE2* **motors past the Needles on the Isle of Wight.**

Chapter Six

The grand tour

You've signed up for a guided tour of *Queen Elizabeth 2* from the top deck right down to the double bottom in the bowels of the ship. You'll need some comfortable shoes as we will be walking a great distance as we take in all the historical changes that have occurred.

OPPOSITE Off cruising. One Deck Lido.
(Michael Gallagher Collection)

The first thing to note is the stairways and lifts. Unlike modern passenger ships with a single class of guest, where the staircases are continuous through most of the decks, *Queen Elizabeth 2* was originally designed for three classes of passenger. The passenger stairways reflected this, serving the respective classes by connecting specific cabin areas to public rooms. This resulted in many staircases being truncated, serving only a few decks. When the ship was delivered as a two-class ship the staircases remained logical, but when open class was adopted their arrangement appeared completely irrational. There are eight passenger stair towers located along the ship's length, designated 'A' to 'H', forward to aft. Numerous dedicated crew stairs are also provided.

ABOVE *QE2* looked good from every angle. *(Michael Gallagher Collection)*

RIGHT 'A' Stairway snakes its way down through the decks. *(Stephen Payne Collection)*

BELOW Signal Deck view until 1972 when the penthouses were added. *(Stephen Payne Collection)*

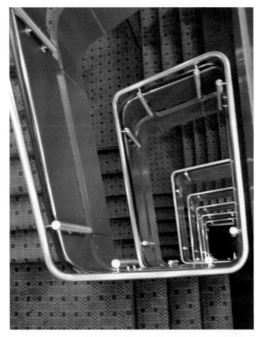

Signal Deck

Signal Deck was the uppermost deck on board *Queen Elizabeth 2*. The lozenge-shaped bridge was located at the forward end of the deck, and was slightly cantilevered forward of the deck below, with swept back open bridge wings. The whole bridge complex was like an island set at the forward end of the deck. The latest navigational aids were provided when the ship was built, and these were successively updated throughout the life of the ship. A control console on each bridge wing was provided for operation of the two bow side thrusters but no controls were available for the main engines or the single rudder; orders were given verbally and were relayed inside the bridge to the control stations there.

The bridge was also the command centre for the watertight and fire doors, these systems being operated from their respective control panels. Immediately behind the bridge was the chartroom where the ship's position was constantly monitored using Admiralty-issued paper charts that were stored in drawers under the chart table. To port and starboard aft of the bridge were two narrow areas put to use as executive offices for the ship's deck department. The whole bridge area was surmounted by a shaped cupola hood which concealed the air-conditioning equipment for the spaces. A small Captain's day cabin was located on the starboard side.

ABOVE LEFT The forward superstructure taken from the forecastle. *(Louis-Philippe Capelle Collection)*

ABOVE Portside bridge-wing view. *(Louis-Philippe Capelle Collection)*

ABOVE The watertight door control panel at the rear of the bridge. *(Stephen Payne Collection)*

RIGHT The fire door control panel on the bridge. *(Stephen Payne Collection)*

BELOW The ventilation fan control panel on the bridge. *(Stephen Payne Collection)*

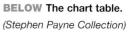

BELOW The chart table. *(Stephen Payne Collection)*

Immediately behind the bridge complex was a raised observation platform from which the mast was stepped at the aft end. The mast rose 61m above the keel and was equipped with two recessed electric Typhon whistles and two platforms for radar scanners, all set to forward. Yard arms and a gaff stay were rigged for flying signal and other flags, whilst rigging was provided for the support of 'Christmas Tree' navigation lights. The mast acted as the outlet exhaust for the main galley, and the venting of this was directed towards the central gaff where the Red or Blue ensign was flown, thus ensuring that the ensign was always gaily flying and never limp and flaccid. The mast originally supported a 1.5m tall satellite aerial, but this was soon removed when alternative technology became available. The lower section of the mast up to the first radar platform was painted dark charcoal-grey, with the upper section painted white.

Behind the mast the top of the deckhouse, like the observation platform, was sheathed in teak. Further aft a raised screen surrounded an open well revealing a sports deck and children's open air area below. The screen was tapered towards its aft end. Immediately aft of the screen was a row of nine skylights that allowed light into the children's play area below. Sitting on top of the aft third of Signal Deck was the funnel house and casing supporting the funnel. The house contained various fan rooms, kennels for 16 animals, radio room, the boiler casing, engine casing and access air-lock spaces to the latter. Large charcoal-grey-painted grille openings at the outboard sides of the funnel house allowed ventilation air to the boiler room below.

The whole open deck area forward of the funnel house was progressively utilised for balcony cabins during the service life of the ship. The first block of ten prefabricated aluminium penthouse cabins was added in 1972 on two deck levels (Signal and Sports). This comprised eight single-deck cabins, which could be combined into pairs to form named suites, and two duplexes (Trafalgar and Queen Anne), which straddled both decks with internal stairs. These were followed in 1977 by two special suites, Queen Mary and Queen Elizabeth, which used the observation platform at the base of the mast as their balcony spaces. Finally, during the ship's re-engining in 1986/87 eight more balcony suites were added to fill the remaining space between the initial balcony block and the funnel house.

Sports Deck (renamed Sun Deck in 1994)

At the forward end of Sports Deck there was a forward passenger observation area with magnificent views over the forecastle and bow of the ship and to each side. The area was protected by half-height solid bulwarks forward and partially at the side; the bridge was slightly cantilevered above and a superstructure deckhouse provided the aft backdrop. The observation area was in fact part of the wrap-around external promenade but was only located on Sports Deck for a short distance, the remainder being on Boat Deck one deck below and accessed by exterior stairs to port and starboard. The forward part of the superstructure was arranged with accommodation for the senior officers, the Master's cabin being at the forward end.

Immediately aft of the officers' accommodation block there was originally a partially covered sheltered teak games deck with a large well opening above, surrounded by the angled windscreen on the deck above and glass screens at the side. This deck was to have been jointly used by Cabin and Tourist passengers, but was allocated to the combined

Transatlantic Class with the move to a two-class configuration. Further aft was a covered Children's Play Deck with the seven skylights above; the Children's Playroom was adjacent at the centre. In October 1972, at the time of the new Trafalgar House management £2 million refit undertaken by Vosper Thornycroft at Southampton, the games area was supplanted by the lower level of the prefabricated aluminium deckhouse of premium balcony cabins. The Playroom, affectionately referred to as 'Noah's

ABOVE Sun Deck aft. *(Louis-Philippe Capelle Collection)*

BELOW Some of the original curved windscreens remained to the end. *(Stephen Payne Collection)*

Ark' in the early years, was designed by two first-year students at the Royal College of Art, Elizabeth Mower White and Tony Heaton. Their design aspirations for the Playroom were tempered by Cunard on safety grounds: multi levels were eschewed, as were ramps, swings, ropes and crawling tunnels with peep holes. The Royal College of Art designed a number of abstract art murals comprising panels of circles and rectangles in royal blue, orange and yellow on a white background to decorate the Playroom. These were designed to inspire expression and children were able to draw on them; as they were easily cleanable they could be used again and again, providing an ever-changing backdrop. Curved fibre-glass screens originally divided the room into different areas, but these were later removed to provide a larger open space. Within the confines of the Playroom were a nursery and a cinema, the latter complete with a sloping floor for good sightlines.

The rest of the deckhouse aft of the Playroom was arranged for Engineer, Radio and Cadet Officer cabins and attendant stewards. The engineers were provided with a small launderette and drying room for their overalls.

The remainder of the deck was a teak First Class open deck protected on three sides by glass side screens. This large area was one of the most popular deckchair areas on the ship throughout her service life. The view forward from this deck was dominated by the funnel and by the ship's name 'Queen Elizabeth 2'

RIGHT The passageway off from 'A' Stairway Foyer leading to the Wardroom, the Captain's Cabin and the bridge. *(Stephen Payne Collection)*

painted on the aft end of the funnel deckhouse, making the deck a favourite place for passengers to take photographs. Attentive deck stewards managed the hiring of steamer chairs and the provision of blankets, essential on spring, autumn and winter transatlantic sailings.

Boat Deck

The Officers' Wardroom and Dining Area occupied the forward end of Boat Deck, being rectangular in shape and spanning the full width of the ship. This was a prime location, and over the years there were a number of attempts to reallocate the space for passenger cabins, all successfully resisted. The Wardroom was sheathed in light wood panelling and incorporated bookcases and at the rear bulkhead a large bar. The dining area was to port, partitioned off from the Wardroom with glass screens. This was where senior officers and staff took their meals. Prominently on display were signed prints of HM the Queen and HRH the Duke of Edinburgh which were presented to the Wardroom in 1970; other decoration included the bell and an engine-room telegraph from the former Cunard four-funnelled transatlantic liner *Aquitania*, 1914–50. Since entering service, memorabilia from the ship's travels were fixed on to the bulkheads for display. Good views forward to the forecastle below were provided by 16 small square windows; additionally there were four windows of the same design to port and starboard. The windows were restricted in size so as not to require storm shutters and to minimise the risk of breakage in heavy weather.

Senior officer cabins were arranged aft to port and starboard of the Wardroom outboard of passenger 'A' stair lobby. The stair lobby incorporated the 'A' Staircase which ran from Boat Deck to Five Deck; this stair was unusual in not being arranged in a fore/aft orientation but spiralling down with flights and landings to port, starboard, fore and aft. For those unaffected by vertigo, it was possible to look down to the bottom of the staircase through the well formed by the receding stairs. Three lifts were provided in line fore and aft, two for passenger use and one for crew. The rectangular lobby extended aft to the forward entrance of the Queens Grill. With access

from the lobby, the ship's Radio Room occupied a space on the portside. In the ship's latter years this was converted into the Caledonia Suite, when dedicated radio rooms were no longer required.

The configuration of the ship immediately aft of the lobby changed significantly after the 1972 refit. Originally the arrangement consisted of a nightclub named the 736 Club, followed by a Coffee Shop at centre and to starboard, and a teenage room called the Juke Box and an art gallery called the London Gallery to port – the three latter spaces surrounding the upper level of the Cinema. The Gallery was designed by Stefan Buzas, who also designed the 736 Club.

During the planning stages for the liner it was envisaged that the 736 Club would act as the joint Cabin and Tourist Class nightclub and bar; with the classes merged it retained its nightclub function in the evening but a small section was additionally arranged as a discotheque for use during the day. The number 736 was John Brown

RIGHT **The London Gallery, Boat Deck port side.** *(Michael Gallagher Collection)*

BELOW **The original 1969 plan of Boat Deck showing the Juke Box, Coffee Shop, 736 Club and London Gallery.** *(Stephen Payne Collection)*

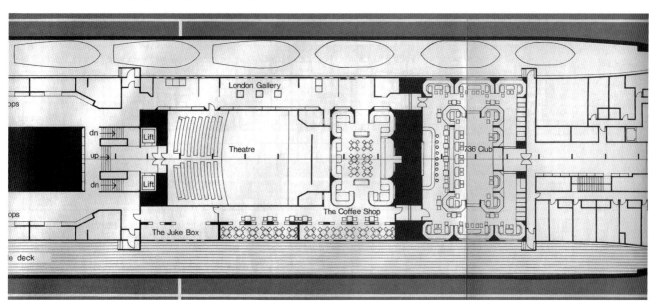

LEFT The Teen Gallery and Juke Box only lasted two years before being transformed into the Queens Grill Lounge. *(Bruce Peter Collection)*

CENTRE The promenade running through the Queens Room, clearly showing how the structural webs were integrated into the space. *(Bruce Peter Collection)*

Shipyard's contract order number for the ship. Much to interior architect Buzas's consternation, hot food and snacks were to be served there, which he attested would change the character of the room. The outer perimeter was two steps higher than the central area, originally conceived to provide good sightlines to the dance floor and cabaret performers. Structural webs formed natural alcoves, and the pillars were sheathed in hardwood with fitted lights in the form of ship's signal lights. The bar was unusual in having toughened glass shutters that could be pulled down over the recessed shelving where the liquor bottles were displayed rather than the normal grille-type shutters. The 736 Club disappeared in 1972 when the Grill Room cabin demarcation concept came into being, following Trafalgar House's first revenue enhancement refit. Trafalgar's concept was to create a three-tiered First Class with standard First, Princess Grill and Queens Grill increasing grades of accommodation each paired with an exclusive single-sitting restaurant. The Queens Grill was created within the 736 Club and the former adjoining Coffee Shop was utilised as the dedicated galley facility. Over time the restaurant was expanded forward to both port and starboard as the number of Queens Grill grade cabins allocated to it was increased by incorporating the officers' duty room and an officer cabin. A feature of the room is a central sunken well with a shallow dome above, decorated with gold leaf. The decor changed over the years but latterly was cream and black; however, a large wooden bas-relief of the crest of Her Majesty Queen Elizabeth II was a constant feature.

The starboard side section of the Coffee Shop and Juke Box, in effect a narrow corridor

LEFT The Grill Room Bar on One Deck. *(Michael Gallagher Collection)*

ABOVE The Princess Grill in 2008, virtually unchanged from the original Grill Room. *(Stephen Payne Collection)*

ABOVE RIGHT Portraits in the Queens Grill Lounge. *(Louis-Philippe Capelle Collection)*

RIGHT The Theatre on Upper Deck. *(Stephen Payne Collection)*

lounge, was converted to become the Queens Grill Lounge. This served as a meeting point and bar for Queens Grill passengers, and was especially popular for pre-dinner drinks that were served from a small bar. A dedicated lift and staircase were installed as part of the ensemble to provide access between the Grill/Lounge and the new premium suites on the above two decks. The London Gallery didn't last long either. It had a variety of functions, including reading room and a computer learning centre, before finally becoming a meeting room called the Boardroom that was outfitted with a long table and chairs.

Cinema/Theatre

The ship's Cinema/Theatre had seating for 491 persons, 136 on the upper level balcony on this deck. The balcony was the preserve of First Class passengers when the

RIGHT Joe Loss and his Orchestra on board *QE2* during the early 1980s. *(Late Edward Divett Collection)*

ship operated in a two-class configuration. Designed by Gaby Schreiber, it was a multi-purpose room used for shows, cinema films, conferences and church services. The main auditorium was created from pre-formed fibreglass panelling. The rear bulkhead, behind which was the light and sound control room, was fitted with slotted acoustic panels to minimise sound reflection. The sound room originally contained booths for simultaneous translations of conferences. The lower seating level was not sloped, but the seating was arranged in a staggered configuration to improve sightlines.

RIGHT Looking up at the funnel from the portside Boat Deck. *(Stephen Payne Collection)*

BELOW The original shopping arcade midships on Boat Deck. *(Michael Gallagher Collection)*

Double Up Room/ Shopping Arcade

When the ship was originally commissioned, the midships portion of Boat Deck aft of 'D' Staircase, outboard to port and starboard of the funnel and engine casings, was arranged as a Shopping Arcade with four shops and associated store rooms. In reality the shops were kiosks, each with a service counter opening out on to the walk-through promenades. The shops were accessible by both classes, First from forward and Tourist from aft. The 1972 refit saw these shops replaced by ten premium cabins, five on each side.

The upper level of the Tourist Class lounge was originally accessed aft of the shops and 'E' Staircase. This was called the Double Up, the lower level on the deck below being called the Double Down, and the two were linked at the aft end by an epic curved stair which splayed out into the open well between the levels. This room was designed by the celebrated architect Jon Bannenburg and was decorated in several tones of bright red. It was a light and airy space because of its two-deck height and an extensive number of windows on both levels. The forward end of the room on the lower Upper Deck level featured a small stage for entertainments and musicians and a large wooden rectangular dance floor. Two bars served the Double Lounge; on the upper level at the forward end there was a large rectangular island bar on the centreline, whilst on the lower level at the extreme aft end of the deckhouse the Double Down Bar had seating arranged in a U-shaped space that encompassed 'G' Staircase. If the ship had remained a three-class ship as originally configured, the upper level of this room would have been the Cabin Class lounge, whilst the lower level would have been allocated to Tourist Class. Sadly, in 1972 the upper level of the lounge on both sides was replaced by a new shopping facility called the Shopping Arcade, which also saw the Double Up Bar replaced by a shop. In 1994 the shops were renamed the Royal Promenade, by which time a sizeable additional shop had been created by enclosing the large previously open raised Tourist deck space aft of the existing shops.

The Boat Deck was sheathed in teak and

ABOVE LEFT Double Down on Upper Deck. *(Michael Gallagher Collection)*

ABOVE Double Up Lounge aft on Boat Deck. *(Michael Gallagher Collection)*

LEFT Double Up on Boat Deck. *(Michael Gallagher Collection)*

LEFT Looking aft on the starboard side of Upper Deck, through the Golden Lion Pub to the Grand Lounge beyond. *(Stephen Payne Collection)*

RIGHT The portside
promenade with the
red-painted rescue
boat. *(Stephen Payne
Collection)*

BELOW The forward
end of Boat Deck with
the climb to Sports
Deck. *(Louis-Philippe
Capelle Collection)*

was a U-shaped promenade that supported the black-painted lifeboat davits that were welded to the deck and the deckhouse sides. At the forward end of each longitudinal run there was a stairway up to the promenade extension/lookout on Sports Deck. The superstructure front on Sports Deck and the Boat Deck superstructure sides opposite the lifeboats were not originally painted white as per normal practice, but in khaki to make the illusion that the lifeboats were floating above the ship rather than being secured to it. This was part of James Gardener's overall styling of the ship. The khaki was replaced with white in December 1983 following the refit at Lloyd Werft in Bremerhaven, Germany. At this time two oversized tenders were added at the aft end of the deck, designed for the rapid tendering (10kts) of 118 people. They were removed from the ship 11 years later in 1994 having been deemed operationally unsuccessful. Tender capacity was maintained by converting two of the lifeboats into dual-purpose tender-lifeboats. As built, the Boat Deck railings were supplanted with a black resin handrail rather than the traditional teak in a nod to modernity and the hope of decreased maintenance. However, these were progressively replaced with teak handrails, and by *QE2*'s return to service in 1987 all the resin handrails had been removed.

Upper Deck

Upper Deck was originally almost exclusively the preserve of Tourist Class, except for the Lookout Bar observation lounge at the forward end of the superstructure, with

BELOW The Lookout Bar, which was only extant for two years, was a popular meeting point. *(Bruce Peter Collection)*

BELOW RIGHT The Lookout Bar 1969–72. *(Stephen Payne Collection)*

QE2 final upper deck plans.

(Stephen Payne Collection)

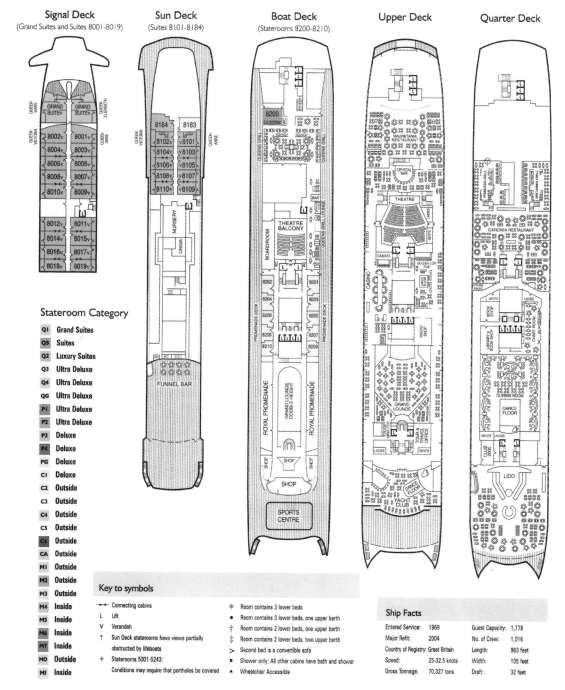

The diagrams and pictures of staterooms shown within this brochure are examples only, and individual staterooms may vary.

THE MOST FAMOUS OCEAN LINERS IN THE WORLD™

QE2 final lower deck plans.

(Stephen Payne Collection)

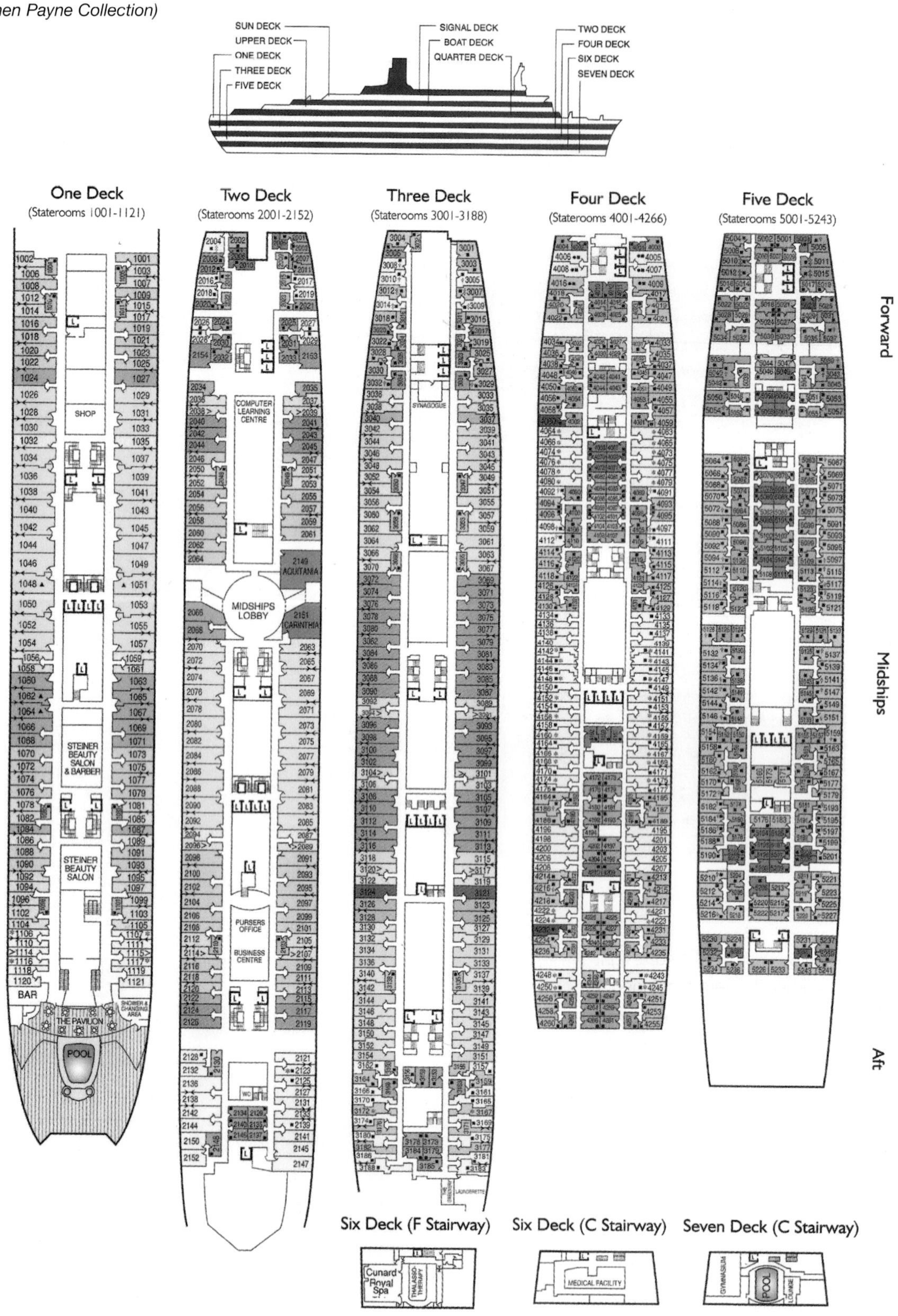

SUN DECK
UPPER DECK
ONE DECK
THREE DECK
FIVE DECK

SIGNAL DECK
BOAT DECK
QUARTER DECK

TWO DECK
FOUR DECK
SIX DECK
SEVEN DECK

One Deck
(Staterooms 1001-1121)

SHOP

STEINER BEAUTY SALON & BARBER

STEINER BEAUTY SALON

BAR

THE PAVILION

POOL

SHOWER & CHANGING AREA

Two Deck
(Staterooms 2001-2152)

COMPUTER LEARNING CENTRE

MIDSHIPS LOBBY

2149 AQUITANIA

2151 CARINTHIA

PURSERS OFFICE

BUSINESS CENTRE

WC

Three Deck
(Staterooms 3001-3188)

SYNAGOGUE

LAUNDERETTE

Four Deck
(Staterooms 4001-4266)

Five Deck
(Staterooms 5001-5243)

Forward

Midships

Aft

Six Deck (F Stairway)

Cunard Royal Spa

THALASSO THERAPY

Six Deck (C Stairway)

MEDICAL FACILITY

Seven Deck (C Stairway)

GYMNASIUM

windows on three sides. This First Class area was provided with a bar on the portside and was accessed through 'A' staircase, which it surrounded on all sides except aft. Designed by Theo Crosby, the decor was distinctly modern, with timber panelling in cedar veneer and chairs and stools in black leather. Spectacular views were afforded through large rectangular windows forward and at the sides. In bad weather, when the ship was pitching heavily, the forward location of this room could see it experience relatively high sea sickness-inducing accelerations. Unfortunately the Lookout Bar disappeared in 1972 after only two years of use when a Britannia galley facility was created within the space, following the reorganisation of the Britannia Restaurant. Whilst this may have improved the catering arrangements, it robbed the ship of its only forward-facing passenger lounge; afterwards only the open deck lookout on Sports/Sun Deck, the Officers' Wardroom, the Captain's cabin and the bridge would have forward-facing views.

Britannia/Tables of the World/Caronia/ Mauretania Restaurant

The Britannia Restaurant was the Tourist Class dining room. Originally conceived with seating for 890, this huge facility was designed by Dennis Lennon and was a world away from the dining rooms on former Cunard liners. Placing the restaurant high in the ship allowed it to be fitted with large windows on both sides, which provided much natural light and good views. Bulkheads were fashioned from fibre-glass in an interlocking tongue and groove arrangement and a vibrant red leather handrail encompassed the room. Seating was set at tables for two, four and six with a mix of single and banquette-style seating, the seating areas being broken up into sections by the ship's structural webs. Models of two historic Cunard paddle-steamers, *Britannia* (1840) and *Persia* (1856), decorated the room. The colour scheme was white, red and blue. The carpet was two shades of blue, royal and a lighter hue, whilst the chairs were made from white Formica with red seats. Galley service for the restaurant

LEFT **HM the Queen meets Britannia.** *(Michael Gallagher Collection)*

BELOW **Charles Moore's Britannia sculpture carved from Quebec yellow pine decorated the Britannia Restaurant.** *(Bruce Peter Collection)*

BOTTOM **Tables of the World Restaurant, 1977.** *(Michael Gallagher Collection)*

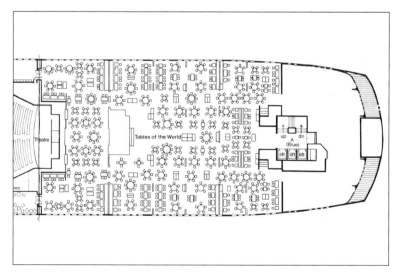

LEFT The Tourist Tables of the World Restaurant replaced the Britannia in 1977. *(Bruce Peter Collection)*

CENTRE Art deco detail of the Mauretania Restaurant. *(Stephen Payne Collection)*

BELOW The Caronia Restaurant. *(Stephen Payne Collection)*

BELOW RIGHT Bas-relief from *Queen Elizabeth* (1940) decorating the Crystal Bar on Upper Deck forward. *(Stephen Payne Collection)*

was provided from the Columbia Restaurant galley on the deck below via up and down escalators arranged on the centreline in the middle of the restaurant. The arrangement was not a success, and in 1972 the new Britannia galley was created within the Lookout, the escalators being removed to allow seating to be increased from 815 to 890 people. Just a few years later, in 1977, the Britannia was refitted to become Tables of the World, five differently themed restaurants in one: Parisienne, Florentine, Flamenco, Londoner and Oriental. Later in 1987 Tables of the World was stripped away and the space was redecorated in its entirety to become the Mauretania Restaurant. Refitted several times, the latest decor was very much Art Deco inspired, being green with wood accents and mirrors. A large circular bronze-coloured aluminium sculpture by Althea Wynne commanded a central location and showed the white horses of the North Atlantic. Two models of former Cunard liners adorned the restaurant – one of *Mauretania* (1907) and one of *Caronia* (1948). For the period 1994–97 the Mauretania Restaurant was renamed Caronia and used as the dining room for the higher grades of accommodation, but the room ultimately reverted to Mauretania and the lower cabin grades. In 1994 the forward section of the restaurant was stripped out and rebuilt as the Crystal Bar, part of the space having been utilised in the interim for a small bar serving the Princess Grill that was installed on Quarter Deck in 1990. In this configuration the remaining Mauretania seated 530 persons.

The Crystal Bar spanned the width of the ship with the bar at the forward end, and was the ideal venue for pre-lunch or dinner drinks. The bar was decorated in an Art Deco style and featured some artworks from the Cunard liner *Queen Elizabeth* of 1940.

Aft of the Crystal Bar the Cinema/Theatre was located, accessed on this level by two side promenades port and starboard. The projection control booth was placed at the aft end of the theatre on this level. The Theatre was designed by Gaby Schreiber and changed little throughout the life of the ship.

The Theatre Bar was one of the Tourist Class's main bars. Situated on the starboard side aft of the Theatre, with large windows with sea views, it straddled the 'D' and 'E' staircases that accessed it. The bar was at the forward end and the room included a small dance floor at its centre. Decorated predominantly in bright red, black and white portraits of movie stars provided decorative contrast and interest. In 1994 the space was stripped out and redecorated to resemble a traditional British pub, with frosted glass screens, brasswork and pub-style furniture. It was named the Golden Lion after the Cunard House flag, which depicts a gold lion.

ABOVE **The Crystal Bar.** *(Stephen Payne Collection)*

LEFT **The portside outside promenade of Boat Deck.** *(Stephen Payne Collection)*

FAR LEFT **'D' Staircase portside on Boat Deck with the Royal portrait that once adorned *Caronia*'s (1949) main lounge.** *(Stephen Payne Collection)*

LEFT **'D' Staircase starboard with Royal portrait that once hung in *Queen Elizabeth*'s (1940) main lounge.** *(Stephen Payne Collection)*

ABOVE The Golden Lion Pub, originally the Theatre Bar on Upper Deck starboard side. *(Stephen Payne Collection)*

ABOVE RIGHT Black and white can never convey the eclectic vibrant red tones of the Theatre Bar. *(Bruce Peter Collection)*

On the portside of the ship, opposite to where the Theatre Bar was located, was originally the Upper Deck Library designed by Dennis Lennon. This was at the time the largest library at sea and a firm favourite, but it disappeared during the October 1972 refit to provide space for a casino. This was originally called the Players Club Casino, and had gaming tables, slot machines and a bar at the aft end. In 1990 the casino was remodelled and extended further forward to include a

promenade area previously called the Casino Hideaway Lounge. A small replacement Tourist Library was provided in the space that was originally the Tour Office. When the ship became Open Class, the former First Class Library on Quarter Deck was retained, whilst the Tourist Library finally became the Photoshop.

Aft of the Upper Deck Library and the Theatre Bar was the lower level of the Double Room, called Double Down. The seating consisted of single chairs, sofas and

BELOW The Casino, Theatre Bar, Theatre, Library and Midships Bar, as shown on a 1977 plan. *(Stephen Payne Collection)*

BELOW The Double Room in the original 1969 configuration. *(Michael Gallagher Collection)*

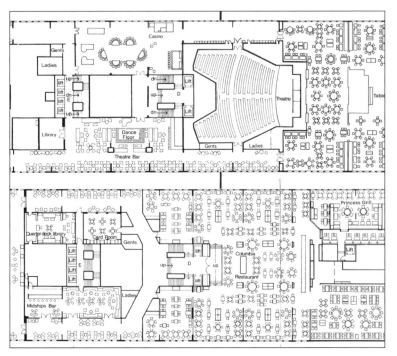

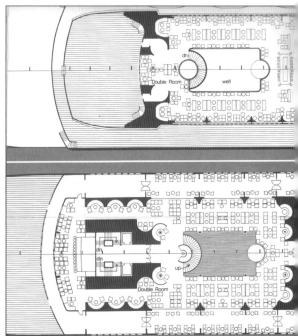

semicircular banquettes set with occasional tables. In 1987 the lounge was completely remodelled and named the Grand Lounge. Towards the rear of the room, seating was arranged on tiered platforms to provide better sightlines, whilst the dance floor could be covered by a retracting carpet to allow further temporary seating to be set out when demand was expected to be high because of special show events. The original aft curved connecting stair between the two levels was replaced by a twin stair arrangement at the forward end, but this was soon modified as it conflicted with the stage and entertainers. Eventually the stairs were dispensed with altogether when a new stair was constructed aft, immediately forward of and connecting to 'G' Stairway.

In 1987 the Double Down Bar aft was redecorated to become the first incarnation of the Yacht Club, the space incorporating the aft enclosed promenade. Later, the room was enlarged by extending the superstructure further aft, at which time it was completely redecorated and internally rearranged with an enlarged bar and a dance floor. Beyond the Yacht Club the teak open deck remained as a prime sunbathing area, protected by curved side screens. The screens comprised trapezoidal windows, of which alternating elements could be partially opened to provide through ventilation.

RIGHT **The Yacht Club looked out on to the aft end of Quarter Deck.** *(Stephen Payne Collection)*

cranes with integral control cabs were originally positioned, one each to port and starboard, to serve the forward No 1 hatch leading to the forward hold. These cranes were of the traditional type with wire operated booms, but the portside crane was replaced in 1987 with a larger and rather incongruous hydraulically operated crane boom, whilst the remaining starboard side original crane was removed without replacement.

The hatch trunk was used for a portable crew swimming pool, which was lifted into position during extended cruises. The original pool was replaced by a more substantial one in 1991.

Quarter Deck

The five decks comprising Quarter Deck and above were constructed of aluminium alloy supplied by Alcad. This gave the ship one more deck than she would have had if she'd been built from steel alone to the same dimensions.

BELOW The First Class Columbia Restaurant. *(Michael Gallagher Collection)*

At the forward end of the deck two 5-ton

Columbia/Mauretania/ Caronia Restaurant

The ship's main galley and the First Class Columbia Restaurant were situated at the forward end of Quarter Deck. This location was

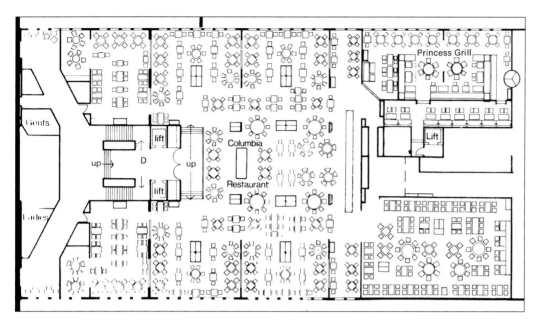

LEFT Columbia Restaurant and the Princess Grill to port 1977. *(Stephen Payne Collection)*

unusual on two counts. Firstly, it was high in the ship, whereas on previous *Queens* these spaces were located low down in the ships; and they were also right forward rather than being amidships. The galley was originally arranged to serve the First Class Columbia Restaurant, the Grill Room on the portside and the Tourist Britannia Restaurant on Upper Deck via the escalators. However, in 1972 it was substantially rearranged when the Britannia Restaurant received its own dedicated galley and the escalators were removed. Throughout the life of the ship, the galley was constantly updated with new equipment. In 1994 it was renamed Mauretania, and again in 1997, becoming the Caronia Restaurant.

BENHAM & SONS LTD: CATERING AND GALLEY EQUIPMENT

The firm of Benham & Sons Ltd was originally founded by John Lee Benham as furnishing ironmongers in 1817, supplying gas light fittings and baths before becoming more focused on providing kitchen equipment. At the time of the *Queen Elizabeth 2* order the company was a respected supplier of catering equipment to hotels, hospitals, the military, education authorities and restaurants. For *QE2* Benham manufactured, supplied and installed most of the catering equipment within the main galley, all to the strict requirements of Cunard, US Public Health and the Board of Trade. It was manufactured from stainless steel with radiused and polished welded joints. Tables had rolled edges and tubular legs that were welded to the deck, whilst sinks and drainers of up to 25ft length

were installed. Panhandler Washing Machines (dishwashers) with a three-minute wash cycle were supplied for washing pots, pans and swill bins. Numerous hot closets with special copper tube heating coils that could be raised for ease of cleaning were supplied, along with fixed steam heated boiling pans of 10-, 20- and 60-gallon capacity.

ABOVE Stainless steel catering ranges within the main galley.

Grill Room

Designed by Dennis Lennon, the Grill Room on the portside aft of the main galley was originally intended to be the modern incarnation of the famous Veranda Grills of the old *Queens*. This was an extra tariff à la carte restaurant with impeccable service and fine dining. The use of the Grill Room changed in 1972 when the ship was reconfigured to provide the premium Queens Grill dining for the Grill Class level of First Class. Whereas the Queens Grill Restaurant was created from other space, the existing Princess Grill was merely retained as an extension to the Columbia Restaurant for that class level of accommodation. This change in function denied its use as an extra tariff facility. Later, during the 1977 refit, the Grill Room was allocated to a newly created Princess Grill cabin grade, serving the mid-range First Class cabins and guests.

The Grill Room was unique in retaining its

red velvet- and red leather-clad bulkheads and layout throughout the ship's life with only minor modification. Originally designed to seat 110 persons, the Grill Room was decorated with four life-size statues representing the four elements of earth, wind, fire and water. They were created by Janine Janet and fashioned from the ocean's harvest of shells, coral and mother of pearl. Access to the Grill was originally restricted to the 'C' elevator, which entered it via a small lobby and a spiral staircase, both from One Deck (below), where a dedicated enclosed cocktail bar was arranged. In 1994 when the Tourist Class restaurant was reduced in size to create the Crystal Bar, the freed-up space allowed the creation of a stair access from Upper Deck to the Grill Room via a new small lobby, off which was squeezed the restaurant's Maître D's office.

As the number of premium cabins was increased there was the need for further Grill Room space, and this led in 1990 to the starboard side of the main galley being rebuilt as a second 'Princess Grill'-class dining space, mirroring that of the portside original. The two rooms were named Princess Grill Port and Princess Grill Starboard, although this was changed in 1994 when the starboard space became known as the Britannia Grill.

The Columbia Restaurant was the First Class dining room and was located directly behind the main galley. Flanked on both sides by full height windows, it was a light and airy space designed by Dennis Lennon and seating 790. The Columbia had mink brown leather-clad bulkheads fore and aft, a pale brown carpet and dark brown Robert Heritage-designed leather chairs. Sections of the room

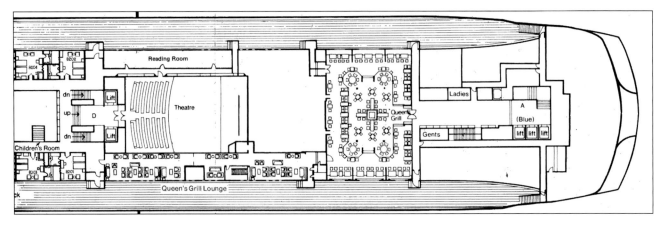

could be divided off for private parties by pale yellow curtains, complemented by the pillars which were clad in pale yellow leather. A distinctive feature was that each table was fitted with a central Perspex tower that was illuminated from below, producing a pleasing glow. The Columbia was used to host many midnight buffets before the Lido Restaurant came into being, and it also had a small dance floor. In 1994 the Columbia Restaurant was completely refitted and refurbished, and was renamed the Mauretania Restaurant. For a short period, the restaurant swapped clienteles when the doors were opened for the budget grade cabin passengers, but this was only a transient situation. When first commissioned, the centre of the room only was used for breakfast at an open sitting, the central tables having pale lemon tablecloths and napkins; whilst for dinner the tablecloths and napkins changed to pink. Meanwhile, the outside tables had ecru linen all the time. The restaurant was accessed through tinted glass doors from a raised deck at its aft end, which led to 'D' Stairway and the lift lobby. This lobby opened out to port and starboard, the central bulkhead being adorned with three large brown tapestries by Helena Barynina Hernmarck that depicted the launch of the ship on 20 September 1967. During a later refit in 1994, the tapestries were displaced by a magnificent cased model of the *Mauretania* of 1907, and they were moved to the top of 'D' Stairway.

To port, the promenade passed the small

ABOVE **The Quarter Deck Library and Bookshop.** *(Stephen Payne Collection)*

BELOW **First Class Midships Bar.** *(Bruce Peter Collection)*

LEFT **The refined Midships Bar on Quarter Deck.** *(Bruce Peter Collection)*

BELOW **The Chart Room.** *(Stephen Payne Collection)*

First Class Card Room and the Quarter Deck Library, the latter being designed by Michael Inchbald. In later years the Library and Card Room were combined, albeit with access through to the 'D' Stairway lobby, the Card Room becoming a bookshop. The Card Room was originally outfitted with panels of green suede and baize. On the starboard side the First Class Midships Bar was arranged. This was decorated in dark green suede and leather with a gold-leaf ceiling and was designed by Dennis Lennon and Partners. As part of the 1994 'Project Lifestyle' refit this space was completely gutted and transformed into the Chart Room.

Queens Room

The First Class main lounge situated at the aft of the Library and Midships Bar was one of the ship's truly iconic spaces. The access side promenades could be integral with the room or separated by curtaining arrangements. The room was designed by Michael Inchbald and incorporated several architectural flourishes including trumpet-shaped fibre-glass sheathed pillars, a large sunken wooden dance floor and an innovative ceiling, comprising a screen with oval cut-outs that were illuminated from behind with colourful lighting. An integral part of the decoration was a bust cast in bronze by Oscar Nemon, which was set within a recess in the forward bulkhead. This was decorated with blocks of walnut interspaced with squares of mirror glass. Inchbald overcame the effects of the relatively low ceiling compared with the main dimensions of the room by perforating the deckhead ceiling with the lattice, the up-swooping effect of the inverted white structural pillars, and by flanking the sides of the room in a specially designed fine wool curtaining with random vertical stripes in white, honey, lemon and pale orange. The carpet echoed the same theme, striated fore and aft with honeyed tones. Plant troughs and cantilevered white lacquered banquettes fitted with interchangeable flame tweed back and

ABOVE The iconic First Class Queens Room. *(Bruce Peter Collection)*

RIGHT The forward bulkhead of the Queens Room. The niche would soon become the home of Oscar Nemon's bronze bust of HM the Queen. *(Bruce Peter Collection)*

LEFT Queens Room 1987 refit. *(Michael Gallagher Collection)*

seat cushions separated the sunken well from the perimeter. Loose seating took the form of seats with an inverted form of the trumpet-clad pillars as their bases.

Originally aft of the Queens Room was the Q4 Room, the First Class nightclub designed by David Hicks. Q4 was the original codename for the ship, with *Queen Mary* Q1, *Queen Elizabeth* Q2 and Q3 an earlier still-born design for a traditional transatlantic-only style of ship. The bar was arranged at the aft end of the room from 1969 to 1982, but following the refit for return to service after the Falklands War, the bar was relocated to the portside, allowing the aft

end of the room to open out on to the adjacent open deck. However, this arrangement was only temporary, as the following year in the refit at Lloyd Werft in Bremerhaven, the bar was relocated and the aft pool beyond was covered with a sliding glass roof called a 'Magrodome'. Q4 Room was eventually replaced by the new Club Lido Restaurant, at which point the sliding roof, which had always been mechanically troublesome, was eliminated along with the Quarter Deck pool. The larger part of the former Q4 Room became the central galley for the new informal restaurant, with the serveries set in a 'V' configuration outboard of the galley.

ABOVE LEFT Oscar Nemon's bronze bust of Queen Elizabeth II painted gold. It now resides in the Queens Room on board the current *Queen Elizabeth*. *(Stephen Payne Collection)*

ABOVE The final form of the Queens Room. *(Yvonne Bauwens Collection)*

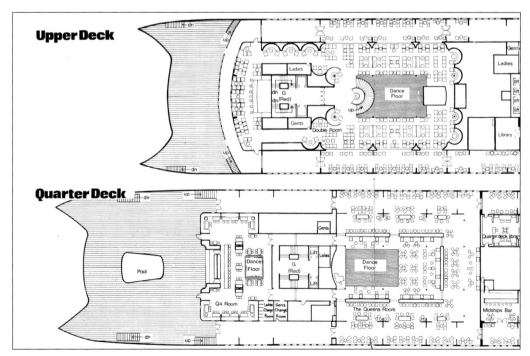

LEFT The Queens Room, Q4 Room and Double Down as shown on a 1978 plan. *(Stephen Payne Collection)*

ABOVE The First Class Quarter Deck pool
and lido set behind the Q4 Room. *(Bruce Peter
Collection)*

LEFT The *QE2* with the Magrodome in the closed
position covering the Quarter Deck pool. *(Michael
Gallagher Collection)*

The original First Class open lido was at first
formed by a teak deck screened on both sides
with large side screens, which gently curved
inwards at the aft ends.

One Deck

The forecastle was at the forward end of this
deck and was arranged with two anchor
capstans for working the forward anchors.
Three anchors were originally fitted, one to port
and one to starboard, both set in recessed
pockets, and a central anchor set in the stem
at the top of the bow. The central anchor was
frequently problematic, as it became firmly
lodged in the stem after wave impacts during
Atlantic storms. Eventually in 1981 the anchor
was repositioned to sit on the portside of the
deck as a spare and the opening in the stem
was plated over. The two anchor chains were
1,080ft in length and had a diameter of 4in,
whilst the anchors weighed 12.5 tons.

A short tripod structure was centrally installed in line with the location where the cables led down to the anchor housings. This tripod supported the ship's foghorn, which was frequently in use off the Grand Banks on transatlantic crossings where fog was a constant problem. The foghorn cone had to be regularly replaced during the winter Atlantic season as storm waves periodically carried it away. The original intention was for the whistles on the mast to be used as the foghorn, but the nuisance this caused to the forward cabins led to the tripod-mounted whistle being placed further forward, where it wouldn't be so intrusive.

The crew galley, servery and mess rooms for the crew grades were arranged at the forward end of the deckhouse. Crew cabin accommodation was also provided forward for female staff, catering officers and assistant pursers.

Passenger facilities ranged from forward to aft along the centreline of the ship included a passenger laundrette, the Grill Room Bar with spiral staircase and lift, the Grill Room above, the First Class Shop, the main fire-station and firefighting control centre, auxiliary and galley switchboard rooms, two room pantries, Ladies Hairdressing/Beauty Salon and Barber. The photographers' darkroom was located forward, and approximately 1,600 photographs per day were processed here from the on-board photographers.

Passenger cabins were ranged along the deck on each side, First Class cabins and suites midships and Tourist Class cabins forward and

ABOVE LEFT The forecastle with anchor machinery and crew life rafts on Upper Deck. *(Stephen Payne Collection)*

ABOVE The foghorn on the forecastle. *(Louis-Philippe Capelle Collection)*

LEFT The Beauty Salon on One Deck. *(Stephen Payne Collection)*

LEFT First Class cabin. *(Michael Gallagher Collection)*

RIGHT An inside Tourist cabin. *(Stephen Payne Collection)*

BELOW The forward mooring deck on Two Deck. *(Stephen Payne Collection)*

aft. A few of the aft Tourist cabins were of the nested configuration; only four inboard cabins for this class were provided. All these cabins were built on board the ship, rather than ashore as modular units, as today. Three pantries provided beverage services to the passenger cabins.

At the aft end of the deck, set upon a teak deck and ranged with similar screening as the First Class deck above, was the Tourist Class pool.

Two Deck

The forward mooring deck was positioned at the forward end of this deck. Here mooring winches worked the ropes and wires that securely moored the ship to the quay.

Another crew mess was located forward, along with a crew recreation room/bar, a crew shop, crew gymnasium, crew library and hairdressers.

To assist with the distribution of baggage throughout the forward part of the ship there was a dedicated baggage handling and storage room. Nowadays, such a facility is deemed a waste of space, but in the days when passengers embarked with huge trunks and multiple large suitcases it was considered essential.

Three entrance lobbies were arranged on this deck along its length. The forward and aft lobbies served Tourist Class, whilst the midships facility serviced First Class embarking and disembarking passengers. The forward lobby was immediately aft of 'A' Staircase and lifts, whilst the aft one was adjacent to 'G' Staircase.

RIGHT The original Midships Lobby. *(Michael Gallagher Collection)*

The First Class Midships Lobby was circular, and incorporated a sunken well with seating and a trumpet-shaped central pillar supporting a circular ceiling. The forward lobby was square and also had seating; this space was later converted into the Computer Learning Centre. The aft lobby was rectangular. The Doctor's consulting room and waiting room were located on the portside, but these areas were later converted into cabins and medical consultations were transferred to the Hospital (later renamed Medical Facility) on Six Deck. Each lobby was served by shell doors to port and starboard, set into the hull to allow access.

Midships, centrally located within the ship, was the Safety Control Room (SCR), from where the ship's safety systems were monitored 24 hours a day. Watertight doors, fire doors, ventilation system dampers and fire sprinkler system alarms featured. The fuel, fresh water and ballast tanks were also monitored and controlled from there, allowing transfers to be made between tanks to keep the ship stable and floating at the correct attitude. On modern ships these functions are installed within a computerised safety centre on the bridge with duplication in the Engine Control Room (ECR).

As on One Deck above, cabins were arranged with the First Class midships and Tourist at the ends, the majority being outsides with only a handful of insides forward and aft.

Towards the aft end of the deck, a Bureau and Office were arranged for passenger enquiries and services. For much of the ship's career there was also a bank, this being operated by various concessions throughout her service life, and nearby there was a safety deposit box centre for passenger valuables.

At the very aft end of the deck was a crew cinema, baggage assembly area and covered recreation deck surrounding rooms containing the official emergency generator and an auxiliary generator, for use in emergencies and during special periods such as dry-dockings.

Three Deck

At the forward end of the deck a mooring machinery and switchboard room was arranged in conjunction with the mooring equipment located on the deck above. Aft

of this were two crew recreation rooms. The centreline of the ship was taken up with much of the air-conditioning plant, distributed along the ship's length to serve the various zones. Also on the centreline were three pantries, a synagogue, cabin broadcast control centre and a crockery store. There was originally a telephone exchange, but when the exchange was automated in 1987 the manual exchange room was replaced by a television studio.

First and Tourist Class cabins were arranged as before, with a launderette for passenger use towards the aft end of the ship on the starboard side, whilst at the right aft were cabins for stewardesses.

ABOVE Tannoy **broadcast equipment.** *(Stephen Payne Collection)*

BELOW Aft end of **Three Deck.**

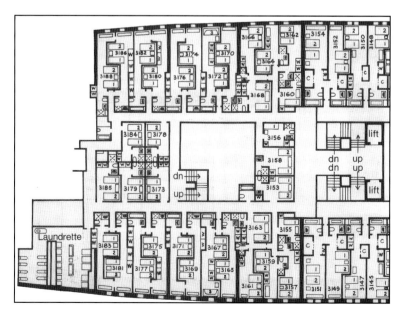

ABOVE **Forward end**
of Four Deck.

When originally constructed, *Queen Elizabeth 2* had the capability to transport about 70 cars via drive-on drive-off facilities, using two special turret-type car lifts, one forward and one aft, that could rotate and move up and down through the decks. This facility was reduced as the holds were used to accommodate an increasing amount of stores, until capacity was limited to 12 cars, and only the forward lift and hold were used. Eventually, the regulations for transporting cars became so onerous because of concerns about latent fuel and contamination that the service was dropped.

Stewards' cabins occupied the aft end of the deck.

Four Deck

At the forward end of the deck was a small store followed by the two chain lockers that stored the anchor chains when these were stowed. Further aft were stewards' cabins and the Quarter Masters' accommodations, followed by a baggage assembly adjacent to 'A' Stairway.

Tourist Class outside and inside cabins occupied most of the deck space, arranged in a much more densely packed configuration than the decks above – many cabins being accessed via dead-end corridors, which wouldn't be allowed by the regulations today.

Five Deck

The top of the forepeak tank is located forward. This tank is used to trim the ship by adjusting the volume of water in it. The chain lockers abut the forepeak further aft, followed by stewards' and seamen's accommodations. A car side door as on Four Deck was arranged to port and starboard, and mainly used for loading stores. Tourist Class cabins densely packed around dead-end corridors and their associated pantries, as on the deck above, occupied most of the space on this deck.

A large stores entrance and handling area

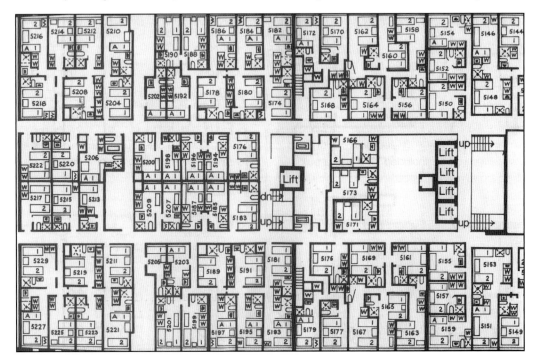

RIGHT **Five Deck**
midships.

via the aft car lift was followed aft by stewards' cabins.

Six Deck

Following the forepeak and chain lockers much of the forward part of the ship was arranged with cabins for stewards. On the starboard side ran a wide passageway which acted as the main crew access along the length of the ship. Other cabins were arranged for engine room ratings, master at arms, catering petty officers, leading stewards and the ship's printers.

The Ship's Office (general administration) was located forward, along with a Tourist passenger launderette that was accessed by a special staircase extension from 'A' Staircase. This facility was later removed from passenger use and was allocated to the crew for service washes. Elsewhere there were a large print shop, general stores and a workshop.

Moving midships there were the boiler room, transformer flat and upper level of the turbine engine room. Further aft came the Six Deck Indoor Pool which was originally for First Class. In 1982 the pool complex was rebuilt as a health spa, with a further complete rebuild in 1993 when Steiners of London won the concession to operate it. The remainder of the deck was occupied by further stewards' accommodation, with the electro-hydraulic steering gear which moved the rudder to steer the ship at the extreme aft end.

Seven Deck

Aft of the forepeak tank the forward part of the ship was dedicated to storerooms of various categories divided between dry and refrigerated types. Included here was a bulk beer store that was a particular requirement to satisfy the thirst of British passengers and crew, whilst a dedicated refrigeration plant kept the cold stores at the required temperature. These stores were unusually located forward to enable easy access to the catering area galleys higher up in the ship.

Forward of the stores an indoor swimming pool and gymnasium were provided. This was originally a Tourist Class facility, and it was transformed into a new spa facility.

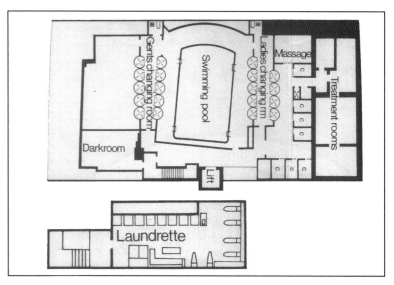

Ranged from forward to aft various technical spaces followed: the main switchboard, the turbo alternator rooms, electrical workshop and stores, the boiler room, the engine control room flat and the steam turbine engine rooms. Further aft there were fuel tanks arranged along the side of the hull to port and starboard, the main linen store and the main laundry. Further aft were Nos 4 and 5 holds that were used for car stowage and cargo – the latter also used as a luggage store, whilst No 6 hold was converted into a waste sorting room in 1987, with waste being refrigerated until it could be landed ashore. This arrangement replaced the original incinerating garbage plant. The tank of the aft pool found on Six Deck was squeezed into the arrangement aft.

Eight Deck/Deep Tanks

This deck was arranged forward to aft with stainless steel bulk beer tanks, the bow thruster machinery compartment, Nos 1–3 forward holds, liquor stores, tanks for fuel oil, fresh water and the laundry, followed by the three main machinery areas, the turbo alternator room, boiler room and finally the turbine engine room.

Double-bottom

The double-bottom tanks were either void or arranged for salt water ballast, fuel oil or fresh water ballast.

Chapter Seven

Operating *Queen Elizabeth 2*

The *Queen Elizabeth 2*, like any great liner, was a complex ship with a myriad of systems and operating procedures. This was all part of the hidden world that passengers never saw. Each day, the ship's passenger routine seamlessly glided from each meal or activity to the next with minimal passenger effort, whilst the ship's crew worked tirelessly behind the scenes. The *QE2* was the first passenger ship to employ a computer to assist with its management, and re-engining brought about numerous advantages that aided operation.

OPPOSITE The *Queen Elizabeth 2* looked good from every angle. *(Michael Gallagher Collection)*

ABOVE At speed in a heavy swell. *(Louis-Philippe Capelle Collection)*

BELOW QE2 pitching heavily in the Atlantic swells. *(Stephen Payne Collection)*

Working arrangements

It was calculated that the ship's average speed would need to be about 28kts and to attain this experience indicated that a sea speed of 29kts would often have been necessary owing to sea and wind conditions. The ship's scheduled speed was ultimately governed by the time required to maintain suitable arrival times at the terminal ports of New York and Southampton, with an intermediate call at the French Channel port of Le Havre. At this speed one hour saved in turning the ship around represented a useful reduction in the average speed requirement for the North Atlantic crossing of 0.25kt. At the high-speed range, with the power-fuel to speed ratio following a cube law, such a small reduction in speed could produce significant fuel savings. Accordingly, a study was therefore made of the baggage handling arrangements at the short stop in Le Havre and a saving of about two hours was envisaged, thus reducing the required average speed required by no less than 0.5kt.

When the ship initially entered service, her transatlantic service pattern largely followed that of the earlier *Queens*, whereby lengthy stop-overs of one to two days were taken at Southampton and New York. These periods of sailing inactivity allowed regular maintenance to be carried out on the three boilers, with each one being taken off line in turn and remedial work being undertaken as necessary. However, when Trafalgar House took control of Cunard in 1971, just two years after *QE2*'s introduction, these stop-overs were eliminated and a much more intensive sailing schedule was introduced. After all, a passenger ship only makes money when she is at sea with passengers, and being alongside with just crew on board is a very expensive luxury. Certainly *QE2* would not have survived the oil crisis of 1973 onwards, when fuel prices soared, without intensifying her schedule, and in some years she was largely

running for her life. The downside to this was that maintenance of the boilers suffered, as they couldn't be easily taken off line: all three were needed in steam to meet the ship's schedule requirements. Coupled with a few unfortunate incidents when feed lines became contaminated with oil, the boiler situation and the reliability of the ship's propulsion plant soon became a serious cause for concern.

Even a variation of a few feet in the position of the machinery spaces had a considerable effect on the strength and subdivision requirements. The position of the main machinery, of course, dictated the siting of the funnel, which was slightly aft of midships. The tall funnel finally evolved after extensive wind tunnel tests at the National Physical Laboratories at Teddington. These included optimising the distinctive forward-facing scoop, which was able to keep the lido decks clear of soot deposits by directing the air stream upwards and thus throwing the smuts up and away from the funnel. Augmenting this action, exhaust air was channelled to fill in the reduced pressure area behind the funnel that was caused by the airflow around it. The lido decks aft arranged in a terraced fashion were therefore kept clear of contaminants under most conditions. This configuration, with the funnel amidships, gave more sheltered deck area than available on passenger ships where the machinery was aft. The terraced decks also

allowed the decks to overlap, thus providing greater lido deck areas and also affording areas that gave shelter from the sun.

Steam versus diesel

In her steam configuration, *Queen Elizabeth 2* took several hours to get ready for sea. Raising steam took time, and if a transatlantic voyage was in the offing all three boilers were required to be in steam. As sailing time approached, steam was carefully fed into the turbines to warm them through so

ABOVE An evening departure of *QE2*. *(Stephen Payne Collection)*

BELOW Docked in Manhattan, January 2006. *(Stephen Payne Collection)*

DEPARTURE

LEFT Alongside the Queen Elizabeth II Terminal at Southampton. *(Blair Skilton)*

BELOW LEFT A shining star. *QE2* at night. *(Michael Gallagher Collection)*

BELOW RIGHT View from the port bridge-wing at departure time from Southampton. *(Blair Skilton)*

BOTTOM LEFT *QE2* is manoeuvred away from the Southampton quayside ... *(Blair Skilton)*

BOTTOM RIGHT ... and out into the busy Solent shipping lane. *(Blair Skilton)*

ARRIVAL

ABOVE Manoeuvring the ship from the port bridge-wing. *(Louis-Philippe Capelle Collection)*

LEFT Dropping the harbour pilot, viewed from bridge-wing (this is at Messina, 6 July 2008). *(Blair Skilton)*

Harbour tugs *Kuttabul* (left) and the *Austral Salvor* assist *Queen Elizabeth 2* to her berth at Brisbane, Australia, 24 February 2007. *(Richard Ward)*

RIGHT Captain Warwick with the pilot as *QE2* approaches port. *(Louis-Philippe Capelle Collection)*

FAR RIGHT Bunkering fresh water. *(Late Edward Divett Collection)*

that they wouldn't suffer from thermal shock when the high-pressure, high-temperature steam entered them in earnest. Upon sailing, *QE2* opened her bow thruster butterfly-type doors and the thruster motors were set in operation, the resulting propeller side thrust easing the bow from the pier, aided by tugs when appropriate if the prevailing weather conditions warranted. Tugs would be on hand at the stern to take the strain. They were almost always necessary there as with no stern thrusters, a single rudder and the fixed-pitch slow reacting twin screws, there was not likely to be sufficient fast-acting applied thrust to effect a timely manoeuvre. Within harbour confines and especially within limited depth dredged channels, the ship's speed

ABOVE Tugs manoeuvre *QE2* into Sydney Cove towards the Overseas Passenger Terminal in 2008. *(Peter Williams)*

RIGHT Four tugs assist with the final positioning of *QE2* for berthing. Sydney Harbour Bridge is in the background. *(Peter Williams)*

was carefully regulated so as not to invoke the nautical phenomenon of squat. This is when a body travelling in a fluid within restricted circumstances can experience bodily sinkage; that is, an increase in draught. It can also adversely affect trim, normally with the stern sinking more than the bow. The phenomenon is entirely due to the flow of water around the hull, the water being accelerated in areas in which it is confined, thus resulting in pressure differentials that cause the sinkage. Therefore, caution was always needed when *QE2* was sailing in restricted water depths, so that she didn't run aground. As the ship increased speed above a few knots, the bow thrusters were switched off and the bow doors closed. Bow thruster effectiveness diminishes rapidly as speed is increased, as the orderly flow of water into the tunnels is impeded. The doors were closed as soon as possible so as not to be damaged by the flow of water around the bow. As soon as the ship had sufficient speed to make the single rudder effective at manoeuvring the ship, the tugs were let go and allowed to return to their base.

Once open water had been reached, speed was steadily increased by admitting steam to more parts of the turbines: an increasing number of nozzles delivered steam to the turbine blades on line with high-pressure steam.

ABOVE The bunker tanker *Whitonia* alongside *QE2* at Southampton pumps heavy fuel oil into her tanks. *(Tony Skilton)*

LEFT Bunker station personnel at work on **Six Deck.** *(Tony Skilton)*

ABOVE View from the bridge. *(Louis-Philippe Capelle Collection)*

LEFT The entrance to the bridge from the starboard side bridge-wing. *(Stephen Payne Collection)*

BELOW The bridge looking to port. *(Stephen Payne Collection)*

ABOVE The bridge looking to starboard. *(Stephen Payne Collection)*

RIGHT On the bridge. *(Louis-Philippe Capelle Collection)*

BELOW The communications console and compass bearing repeater on the bridge-wing. *(Louis-Philippe Capelle Collection)*

BELOW RIGHT Taking bearings with the portside bridge-wing compass repeater. *(Louis-Philippe Capelle Collection)*

This procedure was repeated in reverse when approaching port, slow down being a gradual process before manoeuvring stations were undertaken with tug and thruster assistance. The underlying aspect of manoeuvring in the steam era was the slow reaction time of the propulsion plant. Changes to engine telegraph orders took several minutes to be fully effective, and then any further change incurred a similar delayed action. Apart from the slow reaction of the turbines, fixed-pitch propellers are themselves not particularly effective under manoeuvre. It was therefore essential to anticipate situations and to react intuitively. A comprehensive knowledge of the ship and her manoeuvring characteristics was therefore absolutely vital.

In 1987, when the ship was converted to diesel-electric propulsion, some aspects of these events were made much simpler. Diesel-electric propulsion by its very nature is responsive and quick acting. Diesels can be on line at idling speed and can be brought up to high power almost instantly, with the electrical power so generated acting immediately on the electric propulsion motors to provide a burst of power and thus thrust. The controllable-pitch propellers fitted to QE2 as part of the re-engining were also more effective at manoeuvring than their former fixed-pitch counterparts. Thus *Queen Elizabeth 2* was far more quick acting and much more manoeuvrable as a diesel-electric ship than as a steamship, although squat was still an issue, and she still invariably required some tug assistance at each port of call. It might have been expected that QE2 would have been quieter and suffered from less vibration as a steamship rather than a motor ship, but mounting the diesels on rubber elements and employing a flexible coupling between the diesels and the generators eliminated most of the vibration issues. The new five-bladed controllable-pitch propellers were significantly superior to the original six-bladed fixed-pitch models at high power, resulting in considerably less noise and vibration in the aft part of the ship. Importantly, all this increase in performance was accompanied by a dramatic decrease in fuel consumption from approximately 500 tonnes per day to 350 tonnes.

FERRANTI COMPUTER SYSTEMS

RIGHT Ferranti Argus 400 Computer. *(Stephen Payne Collection)*

Upon delivery *Queen Elizabeth 2* boasted the most sophisticated and advanced computer system installed in a merchant ship. For the first time, a merchant ship was able to undertake a wide range of processing and monitoring functions that had hitherto only been able to be carried out ashore.

Initially the computer performed six primary functions: data logging, with the automatic acquisition of data from the main engines and auxiliary machinery; printing the engine room log; alarm scanning by continuously monitoring the main machinery; and routines for weather routing, hotel stock control and fresh water requirement prediction.

The Ferranti Argus 400 computer was a 24-bit machine employing the firm's Micronor II integrated circuitry. The computer held a suite of programs that it could utilise to perform its functions, switching between them according to pre-set criteria and priorities.

The ship's routine

Queen Elizabeth 2's sea days invariably began during the early evening the night before, when the passengers' wake-up breakfast show was filmed so it could be broadcast the following morning. The Cruise Director announced salient events in the ship's entertainment programme, and this was punctuated with interviews with key members of the crew, celebrities, on-board lecturers and sometimes passengers themselves. Birthdays of the day amongst passengers and crew were announced, as were anniversaries from Cunard's rich history. There were also news items, punctuated inevitably with jokes and humour. The televised show ran for approximately half an hour and was shown on a continuous loop from early each morning.

As the first run of the breakfast show was being screened, keep-fit aficionados exercised in the gymnasium, whilst other passengers were power walking around the Boat Deck. The Lido Restaurant was open for early morning self-service breakfast, and room service was busy delivering tea and coffee and in-cabin breakfasts to those guests who wished to have a leisurely start to the day.

The Queens, Britannia and Princess Grills opened their doors for their respective passengers, who took their seats at their appointed tables. Meanwhile, the Mauretania and Caronia Restaurants opened for open-sitting breakfast, where passengers were allocated tables as they arrived.

Following breakfast, the day's activities got under way. There were lectures in the Theatre from various experts and specialists who spoke about their particular interests; art classes; and voyage one-off specials such as tours of the galley, which were always very popular. Bridge was always an immensely popular pastime, and lessons and games were organised each day. Shops did brisk business, and the Library and associated Bookshop run as a concession by the Romsey firm of Ocean Books were busy from the moment they opened. Once passengers had left their cabins, the room stewards were busy cleaning them and making the beds, replacing towels and other sundries as necessary.

Before you knew it, noon was announced by the sounding of the ship's whistles, and this was immediately followed by the daily announcement from the ship's Master, who gave navigational information, the weather forecast and other pertinent updates. The various bars were busy by then serving pre-lunch drinks, particularly the ever favoured Golden Lion. The popular dance class convened around this time: passengers could learn a new dance and those lady passengers who were voyaging alone could call upon the gentlemen travelling hosts to join them on the dance floor. Lunch was served on the same basis as breakfast, with open sittings in Caronia and Mauretania, allocated seating in the Grills and the self-service Lido crowded as ever.

The afternoon was usually a more leisurely affair, but bridge was still played and further art classes might take place. There might be a fruit-carving or even ice-carving demonstration by the ship's talented catering staff. All these activities led up to Afternoon Tea, which was served promptly at 3.30pm in the Queen's Room, the Queens Grill Lounge and the Lido. This consisted of finger sandwiches, scones, jam and cream, and a selection of cakes and pastries, all served at the tables by a large contingent of uniformed stewards. The ubiquitous cruise staple of bingo invariably followed before the ship prepared for the evening routine. During the day the Doctor's Surgery was open within the ship's Hospital.

BELOW Blowing the ship's whistles at midday. *(Stephen Payne Collection)*

Queen Elizabeth 2 had extensive children's facilities staffed by trained nannies and other professionals. Throughout the day, treasure hunts, puzzles, parties and other activities were organised, and a special nursery looked after smaller babies during the evening, allowing passengers to enjoy their evening meals in the knowledge that their infants were in good hands. The ship also looked after pets on transatlantic voyages, with dedicated kennels situated within the base of the funnel.

Commodity	Daily	Annually
Tea bags	2,500 bags	912,500 bags
Coffee	100lb	16.5 tons
Cooking oil	50gals	18,250gals
Eggs	3,200	1,168,000
Milk	230gals	83,950 gals
Butter	350lb	58 tons
Breakfast cereal	770 packets	281,050 packets
Marmalade/ jam	553 portions	201,050 portions
Bananas	230lb	38 tons
Strawberries	125lb	20 tons
Fruit juice	640gals	233,600gals
Tomatoes	120lb	43,800lb
Smoked salmon	66lb	11 tons
Caviar	6.6lb	2,409lb
Lobster	116lb	42,340lb
Strip loin	450lb	164,250lb
Flour	753lb	122 tons
Rice	380lb	62 tons
Potatoes	694lb	62 tons
Saffron	1.5 packets	547.5 packets
Beer	2,400 bottles	5,309gals
Spirits	180 litres	65,700 litres
Champagne	200 bottles	73,000 bottles
Wine	370 bottles	133,050 bottles
Soft drinks	820 bottles	299,300 bottles
Cigarettes	1,000 packets	365,000 packets
Cigars	41 boxes	12,425 boxes

The evening began with the first sitting of dinner in Mauretania, with passengers being seated at their cruise-allocated tables. Caronia opened for assigned table dining but with an extended single sitting, reflecting the premium paid by guests who occupied cabins assigned to this restaurant; similarly, the three Grills. All the bars did good pre-dinner trade and the casino would be in full swing by this time. On formal nights, when passengers traditionally donned their finest apparel, there might be a cocktail party in the Queens Room. These parties included several Captain's Welcome Aboard Parties (one for each Mauretania sitting, and another for the Caronia and the Grills), where the Captain introduced himself and his fellow officers and senior staff to the passengers.

ABOVE Caronia Restaurant staff sing 'Happy Birthday' to the author's mother.

BELOW The author with his family and friends enjoying dinner in the Caronia Restaurant. *(both Stephen Payne Collection)*

Dancing would be much in evidence in the Queens Room, and later the disco revved up for the night owls. Two performances of the evening show were staged in the Grand Lounge, a film shown in the Theatre, and elsewhere there were performances by pianists, harpists and small acts. Once passengers had left their cabins for the evening meal, cabin stewards made up the cabins for sleeping, preparing the beds and placing a Cunard goodnight chocolate on each pillow. Without question, the ship was a small city at sea, with all the social interactions and amenities normally associated with shoreside found on board.

As was only to be expected, the ship's officers, staff and crew were busy the whole day and night. During the night cleaners were out in force cleaning the public areas, taking special care of handrails to stop any potential outbreak of norovirus or similar infection. The galley was busy, particularly the bakery – where thousands of bread rolls and loaves of bread were baked each day. Later, pastries and cakes were made and advance preparation was put in hand for the meals of the day. The cruise staff were up early preparing for the day's entertainment activities, and concurrently the daily programme newssheet for the following day would be readied for printing, for distribution later in the day to passenger cabins. Overnight, daily newspapers were printed in several languages from news feeds sent by an onshore agency, and these were distributed to the cabins. The Master normally held an early morning senior officers' meeting, where the ship's management could be discussed and any issues addressed as necessary, and then the senior officers subsequently had meetings with their subordinates. If the following day was going to be

CENTRE Painting the anchor chain cable compressors on the forecastle. *(Louis-Philippe Capelle Collection)*

LEFT Senior officers' meeting with the Captain. *(Louis-Philippe Capelle Collection)*

a port visit, the Purser's Office would be busy the night before processing all the paperwork to allow the ship, passengers and crew to enter the port. The Front Desk was also busy throughout the day, with someone always available during the night, for passenger enquiries ranging from on-board accounts, issues within the cabins, lost and found – indeed every conceivable query. Maintenance was on-going throughout the ship, both internally and externally. The engine control room, safety centre and the bridge were manned 24 hours a day and all the ship's officers were busy within their respective departments, ensuring the safe operation of the ship.

In port during cruises, the entertainment staff would be kept busy assisting passengers to their tour buses. If the ship was at anchor, the launches were employed in a shuttle service to the shore. The ship's security staff would in any case be busy, checking passengers' identification and conducting thorough searches of passenger and crew luggage and effects, using X-ray equipment.

The beginning and end of cruises and voyages were always busy periods. On the last night out before reaching port, passengers had to put out all the luggage they wanted landed ashore before 11pm. This was then collected and assembled in holding areas for moving ashore with conveyor and crane. On sailing days the reverse process took place, with several thousand pieces of luggage being brought on board.

TOP Crew muster drill.
(Louis-Philippe Capelle Collection)

ABOVE A Cunard tender takes passengers ashore at Dubrovnik, 2008.
(Blair Skilton)

LEFT Shore leave in Lisbon, 2008.
(Blair Skilton)

Appendices

OPPOSITE Grand parade of three *Queens*. *(Gordon Bauwens)*

1964	
30 December	Shipbuilding contract signed between Cunard Line and John Brown Shipyard of Clydebank.
1965	
2 July	Keel laying postponed because the huge concrete blocks for anchoring the lifting tackle moved when the strain was applied.
5 July	Keel laid on the same slipway where *Queen Mary* (1936) and *Queen Elizabeth* were built. Assigned 'Job Number 736'.
1967	
20 September	Launched by Her Majesty Queen Elizabeth II.
1968	
5 April	The prefabricated block of the wheelhouse is hoisted on board and welded into position.
18 April	The bottom part of the funnel is landed on board, whilst the upper section is added four days later.
19 September	*QE2* boilers are lit for the first time and dock trials begin.
15 November	*QE2* is opened to the public for viewing at the John Brown Shipyard, Clydebank.
19 November	*QE2* sets sail from the fitting-out berth at the shipyard and transits down the River Clyde for dry-docking and underwater cleaning and painting prior to sea trials, under the command of Captain 'Bil' Warwick.
26 November	Preliminary sea trials begin in the Irish Sea, leading up to speed trials off the Isle of Arran.
23 December	*Queen Elizabeth 2* is issued with a Passenger Ship Safety Certificate for the first time.
23 December	*QE2* sails on further technical trials.

RIGHT Docking at Ocean Terminal for the first time. *(Michael Gallagher Collection)*

1969	
2 January	QE2 arrives in Southampton for the first time, and Cunard Line refuses to accept delivery owing to inherent defects with her steam turbines.
18 April	QE2 is finally handed over to Cunard following a successful shakedown cruise.
1 May	Her Majesty Queen Elizabeth II visits the ship for the first time since launching her.
2 May	QE2 begins her maiden voyage from Southampton to New York at 12.45pm, commanded by Captain Bil Warwick.
7 May	QE2 makes her triumphant maiden arrival in New York, accompanied by hundreds of small boats.
1970	
23 March	QE2 welcomes her 75,000th passenger aboard after less than one year in service.
1 June	QE2 concludes a particularly fast transatlantic voyage, arriving in New York after 3 days, 20 hours and 42 minutes, sailing at a speed of 30.4kts.
1971	
9 January	QE2 goes to the aid of the French Line cruise liner Antilles (1953) which is on fire off the island of Mustique whilst on a Caribbean cruise.
5 March	QE2 is disabled for four hours when a flotilla of jellyfish is sucked into the seawater intakes, blocking them.
30 June	Cunard Line and the QE2, Carmania and Franconia are purchased by the Trafalgar House conglomerate, chaired by Nigel Broakes, for £27.3 million.
1972	
16 April	QE2 heaves-to for over 21 hours amid the teeth of a severe Atlantic storm with 50ft waves and 100mph winds, arriving 36 hours late in Southampton.
17 May	QE2 is subject to a bomb hoax and a US$350,000 ransom demand during an Atlantic crossing. Members of the British SAS parachute into the Atlantic to search the ship, but nothing is found.
1973	
14 April	QE2 sails under tight security to Israel to mark the 25th anniversary of the state. The Libyan leader Colonel Gaddafi vows to sink the ship en route, but the threat proves idle.
1975	
14 January	QE2 departs from Southampton on the first of 26 World Cruises.
25 February	QE2, specifically dimensioned to allow Panama Canal transits, becomes the largest ship and first Cunard Queen to transit the Canal.
4 December	The QE2 passes the 1 million nautical miles sailed since entering service six and a half years earlier.
4 December	QE2 sails her millionth mile whilst sailing between Antigua and Boston during a Caribbean cruise.
1976	
23 July	A huge engine room fire travels up the funnel uptake, severely distorting the funnel plating. The resulting damage is evident throughout the rest of the ship's career.
1978	
24 February	QE2 makes her maiden visit to Australia during a World Cruise, calling at Sydney and berthing at Circular Quay.
1979	
2 May	QE2 marks sailing 1.5 million miles with half a million passengers.
1980	
7 March	QE2 makes her first transit of the Suez Canal from the Mediterranean to the Red Sea.

ABOVE **Sydney arrival.** *(Michael Gallagher Collection)*

1982	
25 April	*QE2* is chartered for four days by the City of Philadelphia to commemorate its 300th anniversary.
3 May	*QE2* is requisitioned to serve as a troopship during the Falklands War, and two flight decks are installed at Southampton from 5 May by Vosper Thornycroft to enable helicopter operations.
12 May	*QE2* sails as part of the naval taskforce to the Falkland Islands in the South Atlantic, but initially only one of her three boilers is operational because of defects. After a period at anchor with the embarked troops on board the boiler issues are resolved, and the ship sails to South Georgia via the Ascension Islands, arriving on 26 May.
29 May	640 survivors from the Royal Navy ships *Ardent*, *Coventry* and *Antelope*, sunk during the campaign, board *QE2* for the 6,976-mile voyage home.
11 June	*QE2* makes a triumphant return to Southampton from the Falkland Islands and is greeted by the Royal Yacht *Britannia* with HM the Queen Mother on board.

RIGHT **Arriving in New York. The boot topping was a new type of anti-fouling that was initially only available in blue.** *(Bruce Peter Collection)*

7 August	QE2 returns to service after refurbishing and her hull is repainted a light pebble grey colour, whilst the funnel is painted traditional Cunard red for the first time. The short-lived and unsuccessful reincarnation with grey paint is replaced with black during June 1983 after spoiling of the light paintwork by New York tug fenders when easing the ship in and out of her Manhattan berth.
1985	
18 May	QE2, the RAF formation flying display team the Red Arrows and British Airways' iconic Concorde rendezvous in the English Channel for a prime photo call, using a Hawk jet.
1986	
20 October	QE2 makes her final transatlantic voyage from New York to Southampton as a steamship.
27 October	The QE2 is dry-docked at the Lloyd Werft Shipyard in Bremerhaven to begin conversion from steam to diesel-electric power generation. The 'hotel' side of the ship undergoes major changes, with the Tables of the World Restaurant becoming the Mauretania Restaurant and the Double Room becoming the Grand Lounge.
1987	
25 April	QE2's conversion from steam to diesel propulsion is completed at Bremerhaven, and she is subsequently showcased to the public when she returns to Southampton.
29 April	QE2 makes her first crossing to New York since her conversion to diesel propulsion. Parts of the ship are still unfinished and several hundred workmen remain on board to complete work on the accommodation areas. The ship arrives in New York on 4 May.
1989	
27 March	A consortium of Japanese companies charter the QE2 to act as a hotel ship at the Port of Yokohama.
1990	
22 July	QE2 takes part in celebrations to mark the 150th anniversary of Cunard Line.
22 July	QE2 completes her fastest diesel-propelled transatlantic crossing, averaging 30.16kts over 4 days, 6 hours and 57 minutes.
24 July	QE2 arrives in Liverpool for the first time, the ancestral town of Cunard Line.
26 July	Captain Ronald Warwick assumes command of QE2 for the first time.
9 August	QE2 completes her 500th transatlantic crossing from Southampton to New York.
December	Britannia Grill added to the ship on Quarter Deck starboard, mirroring the existing Princess Grill on the portside.

LEFT Liverpool.
(Michael Gallagher Collection)

1992	
11 June	One of *QE2*'s nine diesel engines (Engine Echo) experiences a catastrophic failure.
7 August	At 2158hrs *QE2* is badly damaged as her underwater hull hits an uncharted shoal of rocks off Martha's Vineyard in Massachusetts during a five-day cruise from New York to Halifax, Nova Scotia. The ship's double-bottom retains integrity, and the ship is subsequently temporarily repaired at Boston before sailing to Lloyd Werft as a cargo ship for full repairs, which cost US$20 million. The damaged area extends for over 300ft with gashes of up to 74ft in length; the keel is dented and twenty double-bottom tanks are punctured. Repair work is completed on 4 October.
1994	
6 June	*QE2*, along with several other passenger ships and a myriad of small boats, participates in the 50th anniversary commemorations of the D-Day landings, with Bob Hope and Dame Vera Lynn on board.
July/August	The passenger bathroom refurbishment programme is under way, successive cabins being taken out of operation while the ship remains in service.
August/September	A passenger cabin and minor stairwell redecoration programme is under way, with the ship remaining in service.
14 November	*QE2* is taken out of passenger service in New York and sails for Hamburg, Germany, with contractors on board who are preparing for her major 'Project Lifestyle' refit; this emphasises the ship's and Cunard Line's history.
20 November	*QE2* enters dry-dock at Blohm & Voss, Hamburg.
15 December	*QE2* arrives in Southampton with a significant number of contract workers still on board.
17 December	*QE2* departs from Southampton on her first transatlantic voyage following the refit amid concerns that much of the outfitting work remains unfinished. Numbers of passengers and contract workers are restricted to 1,000 after the issuance of a temporary Passenger Ship Safety Certificate.
22 December	*QE2* arrives in New York 12 hours late owing to bad weather and is inspected by nine officers from the United States Coast Guard, who assess that the ship made her voyage in a dangerous condition. As a result, the following sailing is delayed by 24 hours whilst numerous defects are dealt with to the satisfaction of the Coast Guard. The incident leads to a full investigation by the British authorities, the Maritime Safety Agency.
1995	
10 September	*QE2* encounters Hurricane Luis on a voyage to New York, experiencing 130mph winds and 90ft waves. One gigantic wave descends upon the forecastle, deforming it and causing damage to the weathertight doors on One Deck, causing flooding in the forward part of the ship including in the crew mess areas.
November	*QE2*'s gross tonnage (a measure of volume not weight) is measured at over 70,000 for the first time, following reassessment of her internal volume.
1996	
2 January	*QE2* achieves another milestone in sailing 4 million nautical miles at sea whilst sailing on her 20th World Cruise.
4 April	Trafalgar House, including Cunard Line, is sold to the Norwegian Kvaerner Group.
1997	
20 September	*QE2* celebrates the 30th anniversary of her launch by Her Majesty the Queen.

1998	
29 March	South African president Nelson Mandela boards *QE2* in Durban to make a historic voyage.
3 April	Carnival Corporation assumes control of Cunard Line and becomes the owner of *QE2*.
1999	
27 February	*QE2*'s first Master, Commodore William 'Bil' Warwick, passes away at the age of 86.
3 May	Marking the 65th anniversary of the maiden voyage of *Queen Mary* in 1936, *QE2* joins in the celebrations with a special commemorative voyage.
2001	
4 October	*QE2*'s Master, Captain Ron Warwick, conducts the first marriage aboard the *QE2*.
2002	
8 January	*QE2* is the first passenger ship to call at New York following the 9/11 attacks.
20 February	The *QE2* resumes her famous transatlantic partnership with British Airways and Concorde, which had been suspended following grounding of the aircraft as a consequence of the Paris crash in July 2000.
14 March	Captain Ron Warwick relinquishes command of *QE2* to take up appointment as Master of the new *Queen Mary 2*, and ultimately becomes Commodore of the Cunard fleet.
29 August	At 2152hrs shipboard time, *QE2* becomes the first merchant vessel to exceed 5 million nautical miles at sea.
2003	
24 October	*QE2* and Concorde pass in mid-Atlantic for the last time before Concorde is retired from service.
2004	
25 April	*QE2* and *QM2* depart New York together on a historic tandem Atlantic crossing. After pausing for a fireworks display by the Statue of Liberty both liners set course for a tandem crossing of the Atlantic Ocean. This is the first time that two Cunard *Queens* have crossed the Atlantic together since the *Queen Mary* and *Queen Elizabeth* many decades before.
1 May	*QE2* relinquishes her role as flagship of Cunard Line to *Queen Mary 2*, symbolised by the transfer of the Boston Cup to the new flagship.
5 November	*QE2* becomes Cunard Line's longest-serving express liner, passing the previous record held by the venerable RMS *Aquitania* (1914–50).

BELOW Two *Queens* meet in New York, April 2004. *(Michael Gallagher Collection)*

2007	
3 January	*QE2* departs Southampton on her 25th World Cruise amid a huge firework display. Seven days later a large Norovirus outbreak affects 28 crew and 276 passengers.
20 February	*Queen Elizabeth 2* and *Queen Mary 2* meet in Sydney, Australia, bringing the city to a standstill as roads are gridlocked with eager sightseers.
18 June	Cunard announces the sale of *QE2* for US$100 million. *QE2* is to be delivered to Nakheel Dubai World in November 2008, where she will cease her role as an oceangoing passenger vessel and be refurbished and adapted for her new home. From 2009, the vessel is to be berthed at a specially constructed pier at the Palm Jumeirah, the world's largest man-made island, to create a luxury floating hotel, retail and entertainment destination.
2008	
6 January	*Queen Elizabeth 2* and *Queen Victoria* sail in tandem across the Atlantic from Southampton to New York at the start of *QE2's* last World Cruise.
24 February	*QE2* arrives in Sydney for the last time.
18 March	*QE2* achieves 32.8kts during a voyage.
30 September	*QE2* embarks on her Farewell to Britain cruise.
16 October	*QE2* makes her 710th and final arrival into New York. Later that day she sails in tandem transatlantic with *QM2*.
11 November	*QE2* commences her final voyage with an emotional firework departure from Southampton surrounded by a flotilla of small boats. Under the command of Captain Ian McNaught, *QE2* calls at Lisbon, Gibraltar, Citavecchia, Naples, Valletta, Alexandria, Port Said and the Suez Canal, en route to Dubai.
26 November	*QE2* completes her final voyage and arrives at Port Rashid, Dubai.
27 November	*QE2* is officially handed over by Cunard Line to new owners Nakheel, to be berthed permanently in Dubai following conversion into a luxury hotel.
2016	
June	*QE2* remains at Port Rashid.

RIGHT On the Clyde, 5 October 2008. *(Michael Gallagher Collection)*

Appendix 2

RMS *Queen Elizabeth 2*: principal particulars and features

	Queen Elizabeth 2	Queen Mary	Queen Elizabeth
Date	1969	1936	1940
John Brown Shipyard construction number	736	534	552
Cunard designation	Q4	Q1	Q2
Port of registration	Southampton	Liverpool	Liverpool
Cost	£29,091,000	£3,600,000	£5,000,000
Maiden commercial voyage	22 April 1969	27 May 1936	16 October 1946
Length overall	963ft	1,019ft 6in	1,031ft
Length between perpendiculars	885ft	965ft	965ft
Beam	105ft 2.5in	118ft	118ft
Decks	13	12	12
Keel to base of funnel	134ft	125ft	131ft
Height of funnel	67ft 3in	59ft	56ft
Height to top of funnel	201ft 3in	184ft	187ft
Height to top of mast	202ft 3in	236ft	233ft
Draught	32ft 6in	39ft 4.5in	39ft 6.5in
Gross tonnage as built	65,862	80,774	82,997
Gross tonnage at withdrawal	70,372	81,237	83,673
Displacement	49,668	78,600	78,600
Service speed	28.5kts	28.5kts	28.5kts
Passenger capacity	2,025, two classes	1,948, three classes	2,082, three classes
Crew	906	1,101	1,190
Machinery	Double reduction geared turbines	Single reduction geared turbine	Single reduction geared turbine
Power	110,000shp	160,000shp	160,000shp
Boilers	3	27	12
Propellers	2 × six-bladed	4 × four-bladed	4 × four-bladed
Lifts	22	20	24
Swimming pools	Two indoor, two outdoor	Two indoor	Two indoor
Radio callsign	GBTT	GBTT	GBSS

Main tank capacities (as final 2008)	
Fresh water:	1,852 tonnes
Laundry water:	489 tonnes
Diesel oil:	207 tonnes
Heavy fuel oil:	4,381 tonnes
Lubricating oil:	336 tonnes
Ballast water:	4,533 tonnes
Boiler feed water:	114 tonnes

Fresh water production and consumption
Four Serck vacuum flash evaporators, producing 250 tonnes each per day.
One reverse osmosis plant producing 450 tonnes.
Total production 1,450 tonnes per day.
Total consumption about 1,000 tonnes per day; equivalent to 14 of the ship's swimming pools.

Appendix 3
RMS *Queen Elizabeth 2*: officers, staff and crew allocations

Senior officers	
Captain	1
Staff captain	1
Hotel manager	1
Chief engineer	1
Purser	1
Cruise director	1
Radio officer	1

Navigation and Deck Department	
Deck officers	10
Deck ratings	36
Deck supervisors	9
Bosun	1
Bosun's mate	1

Engineering Department	
Engineering officers	26
Engine ratings	65

Cruise staff	
Cruise staff	9
Entertainers	5
Dancers	10
DJ	1
Gentlemen hosts	10
Orchestra staff	23
Fitness instructors	1

Ship staff	
Librarians	2
Photographers	4
Florists	1
Hairdressers	13
Beauticians	2
Casino staff	16
Store managers	3
Shop assistants	18
Tour staff	3

Galley Department	
Executive chef	1
Chefs de cuisine	5
Chefs/sous-chefs	107
Crew cooks	2
Kitchen supervisors	2

Hotel Department	
Hotel officers	35
Public room supervisor	1
Administration assistant	1
Bank staff	3
Cruise sales manager	2
Public room steward and stewardesses	25
Bedroom stewards and stewardesses	69
Staff bedroom steward	6
Night stewards	6
Baggage masters	2
Barkeepers	17
Data input clerks	5
Bell boys	2
Nursery nurses	2
Storekeepers	5

Restaurant staff	
Assistant restaurant managers	12
Waiters and waitresses	175
Wine stewards and stewardesses	22
Assistant waiters	9
Lido supervisors	4
Commis waiters	13

Crew welfare	
Personnel manager	1
Crew administration assistant	1

Medical Department	
Doctors	2
Medical dispenser	1
Nursing sisters	3

Utilities	
Laundry staff	17
Linen keeper	1
Printers	4
TV manager	1
Utility staff	182
Secretarial officer	1
Secretaries	3

Security	
Masters-at-arms	4
Security officer assistants	3

Appendix 4
RMS *Queen Elizabeth 2*: some facts and figures

QE2 had 1,350 oval and circular portholes, 577 rectangular windows, 74,200sq yd of chair and curtain fabric, and 2,252 light fixtures within passenger areas of the ship. Throughout much of her service life *QE2* had the most powerful propulsion plant on a non-military vessel (SS *United States* and SS *France* both had more powerful machinery, but the former left service late in 1969, the other in 1974); the most extensive medical facilities after a hospital ship; disposed of all her used cooking oil ashore for reconstituting into animal feed; 277,000 metres of cling film was used every year, enough to go around *QE2* nearly 731 times.

Heineken and Becks lager brands together accounted for almost 50% of the beer consumed on board; pound for pound, the most expensive food item on board was saffron (2.5 times the value of Beluga caviar); the number of tea bags used each day would supply a family for an entire year; to eat *QE2*'s daily consumption of breakfast cereal, two people would have to eat at least one packet a day for more than a year; enough fruit juice was used in one year to fill up *QE2*'s four swimming pools nearly eight times; approximately 600,000 litres of beverages were consumed annually on board.

If all the cigarettes smoked annually on board (6.5 million) were placed in a line, the line would stretch 370 miles, which was equivalent to the distance from London to Edinburgh; on a six-day transatlantic crossing, the following beverages were consumed: gin – 600 bottles (seven brands), rum – 240 bottles (five brands), vodka – 129 bottles (three brands), brandy – 240 bottles (ten brands).

BELOW Moribund in Dubai. *(Michael Gallagher Collection)*

Index